D0201985

Introduction to Ethics

Discovering How Philosophy Shapes Our Morality

Kendall Hunt
publishing company

DOUG CARTER

Cover image © Shutterstock.com

Kendall Hunt
publishing company

www.kendallhunt.com
Send all inquiries to:
4050 Westmark Drive
Dubuque, IA 52004-1840

Copyright © 2017 by Kendall Hunt Publishing Company

ISBN 978-1-5249-1763-0

All rights reserved. No part of this publication may be reproduced,
stored in a retrieval system, or transmitted, in any form or by any means,
electronic, mechanical, photocopying, recording, or otherwise,
without the prior written permission of the copyright owner.

Published in the United States of America

TABLE OF CONTENTS

CHAPTER 1
Introduction to Ethics

"We are discussing no small matter, but how we ought to live."

—Socrates in Plato's *Republic*

Few concerns in life are more important than asking ourselves how we ought to live. Think about some of the most famous people in the history of the world: Jesus, Buddha, Muhammad, Confucius, Socrates, Plato, and Aristotle. What made them famous, attracting millions upon millions of listeners and disciples throughout history? What do they all have in common? They all tried to teach us a better way to live through our moral conduct. They were teachers of ethics and dispensers of wisdom. The reason they are famous is that people are hungry and thirsty for the knowledge of how we ought to live. Why does wisdom appeal to us?

It is often said that wisdom is much more valuable than gold. To make gold useful, it must be refined in fire. As it is melted in a smelter, the pure gold sinks to the bottom while impurities, called slag or dross, rise to the top to be scraped off and discarded. We may think of pure gold as pure wisdom, and the dross as false wisdom, folly, or foolishness.

Arsel Ozgurdal/Shutterstock.com

Why did the ancients believe wisdom was more valuable than even gold? Why did they search for it as for a buried treasure?

¹³ *While I was still young, before I went on my travels, I sought wisdom openly in my prayer.*

¹⁴ *Before the temple I asked for her, and I will search for her to the last.*

¹⁵ *From blossom to ripening grape my heart delighted in her; my foot entered upon the straight path; from my youth I followed her steps.*

¹⁶ *I inclined my ear a little and received her, and I found for myself much instruction.*

¹⁷ *I made progress therein; to him who gives wisdom I will give glory.*

¹⁸ *For I resolved to live according to wisdom, and I was zealous for the good; and I shall never be put to shame.*

Sirach 5:13–18

As we contemplate how to discern for ourselves the decisions we should make on a day-to-day basis, we are contemplating our philosophy. When those matters involve moral decisions, we are practicing moral philosophy, or ethics. But how do we know if we are practicing the correct moral philosophy? In a world that offers such a myriad of conflicting choices, how do we know how to make the right choices about how we ought to live?

The aim of this book is to open our eyes to a candid, nonbiased way of looking at the world and ourselves. Along the way, we will study the teachings of some of the world's most recognized philosophers, sages, and religious texts and test these ideas in the context of past, present, and future world events. In doing so, this book will challenge how we think and help us to develop our own moral philosophy. King Solomon, one of the wisest men who ever lived, urges us to nobly accept this challenge:

As iron sharpens iron, so one person sharpens another.

(Proverbs 27:17 NIV)

It is quite normal to initially find oneself agreeing with several systems of moral thought. At every persuasive-sounding argument, we may be eager, as Emerson says, to "hitch your wagon to a star." Often though, when we test these systems for practical applications we may realize something is amiss. There's a tension inside of us that says, "this particular aspect of this particular moral system just isn't right." That tension is our moral conscience, and studying ethics will help us to align our beliefs with our moral conscience. It is my hope that by the end of the book you will be confidently rewarded with knowing why you believe whatever it is you believe about how we should live.

At the very least, a study of ethics challenges us to exercise our critical thinking skills. One of my former students described studying ethics as "doing mental gymnastics!" Some students find the study of ethics to be quite frustrating; others find it to be liberating. Why? Because we are confronted with ourselves and we are forced to examine the depths our own character.

The only real failure in life is not to be true to the best one knows.

—Buddha

How well do we really know ourselves? When we act in accord with our beliefs based on our moral conscience, we are being morally consistent. When we do not act in accord with our beliefs based on our moral conscience, we can't escape the fact that we are being hypocritical, and something inside of us says that being hypocritical is a bad thing.

KEYWORDS

The word "ethic" comes from the Greek word, *ethos*, which means "character." **Character** may be defined as who we really are both deep inside our heart and mind and how we act toward others. Thus our *ethos* or character reflects the true "us." For instance, sometimes we believe an act is good so we ought to act accordingly, but the reality is we sometimes choose to pursue bad acts instead. The idea behind the *ethos* is that our actions should harmoniously align with our beliefs to enable us to live with a consistent, not hypocritical, character.

Ethics is the study of how we ought to live. How do we align our actions with our beliefs? How do we avoid being hypocrites in our character? Sometimes we just do not know how we should act and we wish we had some guidance. Life becomes complicated. Ethics aims to simplify life by enabling us to act confidently in a given situation. It is more than deciding what to think; it is about deciding how to act.

Ethics relates to all manner of deeds and habits of doing which concern one's fellow men, either as private individuals or as members of institutions-members of the social whole.

—Ella Lyman Cabot (1906)

Ethics refers to the process of determining right and wrong. It is the justification or reason we give for a moral position. Ethics tells us *why* an act is moral or immoral such as, "It is wrong to steal and loot during riots *because it undermines the dignity of others,*" or "It is right to steal and loot during riots *because everyone else was doing it.*"

Morality is the end result of ethical deliberation. It is what we say is right or wrong, good or bad, just or unjust. For example, "It is immoral to steal" and "it is moral to loot while rioting" are both statements about morality.

The word "moral" comes from the Latin word, *moralis*, and denotes a cultural custom. Another way to think of this is that morality is often, though we will see later, not always—defined by cultural norms.

Norm is a term used to convey what is normal moral behavior for a culture. For instance, it is a norm for many Americans when we meet another person to look that person in the eye and to shake their right hand. In many parts of the world this would be considered highly offensive, especially to those cultures who believe the eyes are windows to the soul. Consider an American travelling abroad to India. To show up wearing leather shoes would be a grave affront to the cultural norms of many Indians, since the leather comes from their sacred animal, the cow.

Philosophy is derived from two Greek words: *philos*, meaning the love of something, and *sophia*, or wisdom. Thus, philosophy is the study of, or love of wisdom. Ethics is the branch of philosophy known as moral philosophy.

Moral philosophy, then, is a study which aims to answer the question, "What is the wise way to live?" The primary goal or purpose of studying ethics is to learn to discern truth from error. What is the truth about right or wrong, good or bad, just or unjust? If we know what is true, and we live accordingly, we can live wisely and consistently.

TYPES OF ETHICS

Ethics may be categorized into various types:

Descriptive ethics attempts to describe the actual normal behavior for societies. Why do some cultures bury their dead, some burn them, and yet others eat specific body parts of deceased family members? Descriptive ethics provides a framework of reason for the accepted and rejected moral standards for a society.

Normative ethics prescribes normative behavior for a society. When most people debate about ethics, they are typically trying to decide what the standard normative behavior ought to be. Should marriages be arranged by parents? At what age should people be permitted to marry? Should marijuana be legalized? Should abortion be legalized, and if so, under what conditions?

Metaethics attempts to define what is meant by such terms as "good," "evil," "right," "just," "unjust," "happiness," "truth," "freedom," and so on. Metaethics also seeks to reveal such things as the origin of basic philosophical principles, universal or absolute truths, and the will of the Divine in the governance of mankind and the world.

Aretaic ethics, also called "virtue theory" is concerned with the virtues and character produced in people. Aretaic ethics questions the motivation of moral actions. Did the moral agent do a particular act out of a good will, or because the agent was forced to do so? Aristotle's *Nicomachean Ethics* and Ayn Rand's rational egoism are examples of virtue-based ethical theories.

Deontological (from the Greek word, *deon* meaning "duty") **ethics** are types of normative ethics that are concerned with developing rules or following certain obligations as standards for ethical conduct. According to deontological theories, the agent who follows established rules as if they were one's moral duty is acting morally. Immanual Kant espouses such a deontological position as do countless religions.

Teleological (from the Greek word, telos, meaning "end" or "goal") **ethics** are types of normative ethics that insists the rightness or wrongness of a particular act is determined by the goodness or badness of the consequences of that action. If the action turned out to be beneficial, then it must have been a good act. If the action resulted in a bad consequence, then the action must have been a bad act. An example of teleological thinking is the phrase, "It's not wrong if you don't get caught!" Two other examples of teleological ethics that we will examine in later chapters are egoism and utilitarianism.

Consequential ethics are concerned about determining the right course of action from an analysis of the consequences of an action. Teleological ethics is a consequentialist theory. If we let immigrants come in from nations that are hostile to US citizens, could this threaten the security of the nation? Was the bombing of Hiroshima and Nagasaki with atomic bombs justified even though it led to the end of World War II?

Nonconsequentialist ethics include those ethical theories that are not concerned with determining the right course of action from an analysis of the consequences of an action. Instead, the rightness or wrongness of an action depends on other factors such as the intent of the person doing the moral act, or the fulfilment of duties and obligations inherent to the cause of justice. Deontological ethics is a nonconsequentialist moral theory.

THE VALUE OF WISDOM

Throughout history, cultures around the globe have sought to collect and preserve wisdom for future generations. Like most other known indigenous peoples, the wisdom of the Australian Aboriginals is passed down in oral tradition in the form of myths. One must learn the stories well, because they possess the wisdom needed to survive in the harsh Australian outback. Although you the reader may not be seeking wisdom for survival in the outback, figuratively speaking from time to time you may find yourself struggling to survive in a wilderness period of your own life. A study of ethics will help prepare you for such a time.

Wisdom Transcends Time, Culture, and Geography

Essentially, what we discover is that every known human civilization has sought to understand how to live wisely. Certainly not every individual, mind you, but at least every civilization has thought about what might be the best way to live and has developed some sort of ethical guideline to meet this need.

In India, the *Upanishads* are a collection of sacred philosophical scriptures of the Hindu religion. Collected approximately between 600 and 100 BC, these are primarily dialogues between teachers and young students seeking sacred knowledge. Why is this knowledge considered sacred, you ask? One of the most important aspects of the Upanishads is its perceived usefulness for attaining *jnana*, an enlightening form of spiritual wisdom which awakens and transforms one's consciousness or Self. In Hindu thought, the Self hinders one from attaining harmony with Reality.

Prior to the most ancient teachings within the *Upanishads*, the Jewish people compiled their own set of wisdom books. One of these, called *Proverbs*, was compiled sometime between 729 and 686 BC. The proverbs also contain short, memorable sayings to aid in wisdom. The second and third proverbs contain the words of a father imploring his son to seek wisdom:

> *My son, if you accept my words and store up my commands within you, turning your ear to wisdom and applying your heart to understanding, and if you call out for insight and cry aloud for understanding, and if you look for it as for silver and search for it as for hidden treasure ... then you will understand what is right and just and fair-every good path ... discretion will protect you and understanding will guard you ... Blessed is the man who finds wisdom, the man who gains understanding, for she is more profitable than silver and yields better returns than gold, she is more precious than rubies; nothing you desire can compare with her.*

> (Proverbs 2:1–4, 9, 11 and 3:13–15 NIV)

The ancient Persians who lived in what is now Iran were once known for their wisdom in respect for other cultures. Evidence for this fact is recorded on the Cyrus Cylinder found in the ancient city of Babylon, and later in the biblical story of the wise men who travelled from the East to visit a young Jewish child named Jesus, bringing him the elaborate, yet symbolic gifts of gold, frankincense, and myrrh.

The Cyrus Cylinder

The Cyrus Cylinder is a small, clay cylinder with an inscription written in cuneiform that was excavated from the ruins of the ancient city of Babylon in modern-day Iraq. Sometimes referred to as "the first declaration of human rights," the Cyrus Cylinder is a proclamation from the Persian King Cyrus (c. 559–530 BC) to allow the Babylonian citizens to worship their own gods rather than require them to worship the gods of their Persian conquerors. A similar story is found among the people of Israel in 2 Chronicles 36:22–23:

"Now in the first year of Cyrus king of Persia in order to fulfill the word of the Lord by the mouth of Jeremiah, the Lord stirred up the spirit of Cyrus king of Persia, so that he sent a proclamation throughout his kingdom, and also put it in writing, saying, "Thus says Cyrus king of Persia, 'the Lord, the God of heaven, has given me all the kingdoms of the earth, and He has appointed me to build Him a house in Jerusalem, which is in Judah. Whoever there is among you of all His people, may the Lord his God be with him, and let him go up!'"

(NASV)

In ancient Greece, philosophical schools devoted to the instruction of wise living were common. There, we find the schools of Pythagoras, Socrates, Plato, Aristotle, Epicurus, and many others.

Pythagoras (c. 569–475 BC), whom we give credit for the Pythagorean Theorem in geometry, travelled to Egypt in pursuit of their wisdom in math and religion, particularly their geometry and cosmology. Apparently, Pythagoras was encouraged by Thales of Miletus (c. 524–547 BC), who is known as the first Greek philosopher, mathematician, and scientist. Pythagoras was also influenced by a student of Thales named Anaximander (c. 610–546 BC), who became known as the first Greek astronomer and founder of Greek cosmology.

Confucius' *Analetics* also aspires to teach wise ways to live. Written near the latter years of Pythagoras' life, around 479 BC in China, *Analetics* is essentially a collection of proverbs or short statements spoken by Confucius and his disciples aimed at teaching easily memorable bits of wisdom. Among the contents of *Analects* one will discover ethical discussions on such topics including faithfulness or reliability (*xin*), loyalty (*zhong*), righteousness (*yi*), valor (*yong*), and virtue (*de*). Analects also contains discussions about living a morally ideal life (*junzi*) and descriptions of what the morally ideal life might look like (*ren*):

The Master (Confucius) said, To settle in ren *is the fairest course. If one chooses not to dwell amidst* ren, *whence will come knowledge?*

(Analects, Book IV, 4.1)

The Master (Confucius) said, Those who are not ren *cannot long dwell in straitened circumstances, and cannot long dwell in joy. The* ren *person is at peace with* ren*. The wise person makes use of* ren*.*

(Analects, Book IV, 4.2)

The Master said, … "If one takes ren *away from a junzi, wherein is he worthy of the name? There is no interval so short that the junzi deviates from* ren*. Though rushing full tilt, it is there; though head over heels, it is there."*

(Analects, Book IV, 4.5)

The various tribes of American Indians have a rich tradition in wisdom. According to tradition, in 1887 a Lakota Sioux Chief named Yellow Lark translated a prayer for wisdom into English. He wrote:

"Oh, Great Spirit, whose voice I hear in the wind,

whose breath gives life to all the world- hear me.

I need your strength and wisdom. Let me walk

in beauty, and make my eyes ever behold

The red and purple sunset.

Make my hands respect the things you have made

and my ears sharp to hear your voice.

Make me wise so that I may understand

The things you have taught my people.

Help me to remain calm and strong in the face

of all that comes towards me.

Let me learn the lessons you have hidden in every leaf and rock.

Help me seek pure thoughts and act with the intention of helping others.

Help me find compassion without empathy overwhelming me.

I seek strength, not to be greater than my brother,

but to fight my greatest enemy—myself (my fears and my doubts).

Make me always ready to come to you with clean hands

and straight eyes. So when life fades, as the fading sunset,

my spirit may come to you without shame.

Wisdom comes when you start living the life the Creator intended for you.

Native American proverb

As much as it is a study of wise living, moral philosophy is also a study of Truth. This, of course, implies that there is an absolute reality. But just what is this truth? Theoretically, Truth is Reality, and philosophy is very concerned with determining what is real. What we are after then, is the very source of wisdom. From where does wisdom come? Can we point to a beginning of wisdom, or is wisdom eternal? To answer these questions, we must turn again to the world's most ancient civilizations and read into their myths. Each of these civilizations contributes interesting details to a story about wisdom that knits the world together, and these stories often discuss the preexistence of wisdom before the world was created.

The Origin of Moral Wisdom

It is one thing to recognize that cultures around the world and throughout time have so greatly treasured wisdom, but something altogether different to actually acquire and to apply that wisdom to ourselves. Moreover, it is likewise important to recognize the importance of applied wisdom not only in our daily lives, but also in the context of our society's place alongside our neighboring societies throughout the world.

The oldest civilizations on earth—those considered to be the indigenous peoples to an area—appear to have the most simple ethical practices and the most well-thought-out religious convictions. They taught their ethics with myths, practice, symbols, architecture, and ceremonies. They built raised areas upon which they could be closer to the heavens. Even today, these raised areas are still in existence. These are the ancient pyramids that can be found all over the globe—from Egypt to Europe to India to China to Central and South America. In North America, earthen pyramids are common. Interestingly, they each share some connection to a religious function, and their stories are closely tied with the acquisition and application of wisdom.

Applying Moral Wisdom

A study of ethics typically includes various theories of reality, which can be used to help us answer questions such as: What do we mean by "good" or "evil"? What is "right" or wrong"? How do we determine what is "just" or "unjust"? It is not enough to just debate those terms. Moral wisdom yearns to be applied.

Ethics helps us to answer questions such as:

Is the world overpopulated? If it is, what should we do about it? Should I plan to have as many children as I want? Should governments enact a child-limiting policy such as China's one-child policy? What if the world isn't overpopulated? Could it ever be?

Should we allow fourth trimester abortions? In class, I like to show a video of a man on a college campus collecting signatures for a petition to allow fourth trimester abortions. It's fun to watch the reactions of students as they gradually catch on to what the guy is actually doing. After all, there are only three trimesters before a baby is born; the fourth trimester is the three-month period *after* the baby is born.

Should nurses be allowed to perform abortions?

Is it right for the government to force males to buy insurance that includes female contraceptives? Should the government force females to buy insurance that includes male contraceptives? Should the government force anyone to buy anything at all?

Should the Second Amendment be overturned—stripping away the right to keep and bear guns? Why are opinions about this topic so hotly debated?

Moral Authorities

Is something right or wrong just because we think it is so? Can anything and everything really be right for one, yet wrong for another? How do we know? What drives us to make the moral decisions that we make?

A **moral authority** is a source to which one appeals to justify his/her moral behavior. All moral judgments are made based on a moral authority, so to understand someone, or even ourselves, we should learn to recognize the authority or combination of authorities being expressed. There are five sources of moral authority: reason, tradition, history, experience, and divine revelation.

Reason is the attempt to make rational decisions based on a careful calculation of evidences and facts. We observe and make judgments upon our observations.

Tradition is the authority which maintains the time-honored status quo. Typically, those who hold to tradition as a primary moral authority are reluctant to change and adapt to new circumstances and information. Tradition says, "We've always done it this way, so this way is right and best."

History enables us to make rational claims based on established precedences.

The more you know about the past, the better prepared you are for the future.

—Theodore Roosevelt

Those who don't know history are destined to repeat it.

—Edmund Burke

If all human beings understood history, they might cease

making the same stupid mistakes over and over.

—Isaac Asimov

Life must be lived forward, but it can only be understood backward.

—Soren Kierkegaard

Experience is a moral authority with respect to that which we understand through experience to be true.

I have but one lamp by which my feet are guided, and that is the

lamp of experience. I know no way of judging of the future but by the past.

—Patrick Henry

Divine Revelation includes religious texts and other proclamations by those with religious authority such as prophets who speak on behalf of the Divine.

Recognizing Moral Authority/Worldviews

Why is it important to recognize moral authority when we engage in ethical conversations (a.k.a. arguments)? It helps to explain one's worldview. If we have an understanding of one's worldview, we can question or test the conclusions reached.

A **worldview** is simply the way in which a person views the world and his place in the world. It is very difficult for a religious person using divine revelation as their source of moral authority to sway an opinion of a nonreligious person. Likewise, it is very difficult to use rational arguments to persuade members of a culture that allow adult–child marriages that such a form of pedophilia is not acceptable. Such tradition is often fused in religious beliefs as well, making the task of persuasion that much more difficult.

Again, we are faced with the burden of deciding how we ought to live. In Chapter 2, we will examine formal ways in which we can test our own moral opinions as well as the moral opinions of others.

CHAPTER 2
Critical Thinking and Ethics

Reasons are the pillars of the mind.

—Edward Counsel

Any studious discussion about living wisely should include a study of thinking wisely and identifying worldviews. In this chapter, we explore what this means, we learn how to think wisely for ourselves, and we learn to recognize unwise or unclear thinking patterns.

Our moral convictions are based on reasons. If reasons are the pillars of the mind, or our moral convictions, then it is important to test the strength of our mental pillars. After all, we wouldn't trust a bridge over a body of water unless we are confident that the bridge has been thoroughly tested and its integrity proven. Likewise, wise living involves solid, correct thinking, and acting.

We must be committed to searching ourselves for honesty. To think honestly, we must ask, "Is my belief about this matter consistent with what I profess about other matters?" "Am I prepared to dismiss a belief I once held?" "Could my moral authority (reason, tradition, experience, history, or divine revelation) ever be wrong or misinterpreted?" "Are my beliefs honestly justified?"

Honesty is the first chapter in the book of wisdom.

—Thomas Jefferson

Honest thinking requires correct thinking, and correct thinking follows certain rules. These rules of thinking are discussed in the branch of philosophy called logic. When we engage in ethical debates, it is essential that we think correctly.

Logic is the science and art of thinking correctly. It is a science because it follows a pattern of logical truths and principles governing correct thinking. Recall the five steps of the scientific method. What are they? (1) Observe the world around us, including the moral world; (2) form a question about your observation; (3) form a hypothesis; (4) conduct an experiment; and (5) analyze the data and draw a conclusion.

Logic is also a form of art. In art classes, we learn to design and to construct and to form things. Logic is an art in the sense that we design and form good arguments based on well-constructed patterns of thought.

Beware of false knowledge; it is more dangerous than ignorance.

—George Bernard Shaw

The term "logic" comes from the Greek word, *logos*, meaning "word," "reason," or "plan." To the ancient Greeks, the logos was the rational structure of the world. They believed that implicit to the cosmos was a preexisting reality that operated on the principles of absolutes. Therefore, it isn't surprising to see why Pythagoras travelled to Egypt to study their cosmology.

In the Bible, the book of John borrows this concept:

> *In beginning was the* logos, *and the* logos *was with God, and God was the* logos.

John 1:1

This is translated more fully into English like so:

> *In the beginning was the Word, and the Word was with God and God was the Word.*

The ancient people of India had a very similar concept called *rita*. Rita, which is found in Hinduism's sacred *Vedas* (compiled c. 1500–1000 BC), means "truth" or "order." Specifically, rita refers to a cosmic order that encompasses a physical order, a moral order, and a religious order. Together, these are all necessary parts of the reality or truth of that which *is*, or the essence of *beingness*.

Logical thinking evaluates statements, or claims, based on their truth value. Logical thinking habitually asks the questions, "Am I thinking correctly?" "Is the statement true or is it false?" For example, if I say, "It is cold outside," or "This lasagna tastes really good," I'm making a statement that is either true or false. The same may be said of the following statements: "The world is over-populated," or "The world is not-overpopulated," and "Man-caused climate change is real," or "Man-caused climate change is not real." Notice that in the last set of examples, the truth claims conflict. These can't all be true.

As we read in Chapter 1, **reality** is that which is true. Logical thinking is concerned with finding out truth. Therefore, logical thinking guides us in our search for reality. The goal of thinking critically is to lead us to a full and complete understanding of the reality of a matter.

Logic and critical thinking skills enable us to "uproot and tear down, to destroy and overthrow" faulty beliefs, and "to build and to plant" in their place beliefs grounded in truth that is justified (Jeremiah 1:10). Elsewhere, the Bible affirms the principles of logical thinking to demolish strongholds (including those of thought patterns), arguments, and falsehoods.

> *The weapons we fight with are not the weapons of this world. On the contrary, they have divine power to demolish strongholds. We demolish arguments and every pretension that sets itself up against the knowledge of God, and we take captive every thought to make it obedient to Christ.*

—2 Corinthians 10:4–5 (NIV)

Propositions are special types of sentences which make claims of truth or falsity. Think of a basic sentence structure with a simple subject, verb (called a copula in formal logic) and a predicate. A typical proposition looks like this: "The sun is bright."

Induction reasoning starts with facts, or particulars, and moves toward a general or probable conclusion. For example, a mother observes that her daughter's new boyfriend drives a dirty car, plays his music too loudly in the neighborhood, does not address adults with the usual titles of respect (i.e., sir or ma'am, Mr., Ms., or Mrs.), does not have a job, and never offers to help clean up the kitchen after eating dinner with her family. She is thus likely to conclude that her new daughter's boyfriend is probably not a very good choice.

Deductive reasoning is another way of thinking that begins with generalities and moves toward a definitive conclusion. Using the scenario earlier, the mother might reason in this manner:

All (boyfriends) who never cleans his car are not a responsible car owner.
(Boyfriend) never cleans his car.
Therefore, (boyfriend) is not a responsible car owner.
Again,
All (boyfriends) that play music too loudly in the neighborhood are inconsiderate of others.
(Boyfriend) plays his music too loudly in the neighborhood.
Therefore, (boyfriend) is inconsiderate.

LOGICAL FALLACIES

Learn what is true in order to do what is right.

—Thomas Huxley

Sometimes, the opinions we hold are not based on truth. How do we discern what is true from that which is not true? One way is by examining evidences. We must ask ourselves, "Am I ignoring evidences—true claims—which would alter my opinion?

Another way to discern what is true from what is not true is to pick out errors in thinking. Errors in thinking are also known as logical fallacies such as the ones below.

Ad Hominem

Have you ever really listened to those people that belittle or try to shout down anyone who disagrees with their opinion? They often present *ad hominem* attacks which look more like verbally throwing sticks, stones, rubber ducks, and whatever else they can find in the heat of the moment to attack their opponent's character. Ad hominem literally means, "against the person," and is a direct personal attack against an opponent.

The ad hominem fallacy is easy to spot; it's characterized by insults and threats such as "you're so stupid," or "they're just ignorant fools." Sometimes it's wiser to walk away from a fool than to engage in his folly.

Talk sense to a fool and he calls you foolish.

—Euripides, *The Baccae* (480–406 BC)

He who threatens us will find us deaf to his threats.

We are willing to listen only to rational arguments.

—Menachem Begin

Appeal to Authority

An appeal to authority fallacy is marked by an appeal to an authority figure to win you over. A 1960s era television commercial asks the question, "Which brand of cigarette do you smoke, doctor?" and answers that question with, "More doctors smoke Camels than any other cigarette."

Appeal to Emotion

When someone attempts to persuade an opinion with the use of emotional language, and at the expense of rational thinking, the attempt is called an appeal to emotion. The fallacy occurs when a rational conclusion contradicts the validity or soundness of the argument. Adolph Hitler understood the power of emotional rhetoric to easily manipulate large numbers of people. He explained, *"The broad masses of a population are more amenable to the appeal of rhetoric than to any other force."* He then used this tactic to persuade his people that purifying the human genepool to create a superior human race by killing anyone deemed to be an inferior human was in the best interest of mankind.

Appeal to the Crowd (*ad populum*)

Generally speaking, people feel uncomfortable if we have the impression that we don't "fit in" with the crowd. We also tend to feel uncomfortable at the thought that others may think we are ignorant if we express a differing opinion. Thus, to many people, it is easier to go along with the crowd than it is to stand on one's own feet. The Appeal to the Crowd fallacy exploits this emotion and insists that the crowd is always right, and those who disagree with the crowd hold an intellectually inferior opinion. When directed at peace-loving people, the appeal to the crowd fallacy is also quite effective at limiting the voice of a rival opinion. But is the crowd always right?

Even if you are a minority of one, the truth is the truth.

—Mahatma Gandhi

Appeal to Force

The appeal to force is a common problem characterized by the use of threats or intimidation to get a conclusion accepted. I spent much of my twenties managing golf courses. Most of that time was in beautiful, sunny, south Florida, where it also happened to rain every afternoon. The afternoon rains meant that work days were frequently cut short, and therefore work was carried over to the next day. The rains also made it more challenging to complete tasks by promised deadlines. To help ensure progress toward predetermined goals, my superiors occasionally insisted that I demand employees under my supervision work unannounced overtime. Thus, I quickly learned the appeal to force tactic. If I somehow didn't find a way to get the work done, I knew that I'd be out of a job that I desperately needed, and I was forced to force others to experience the same pressure I felt. I'm not condoning the action, but at the time I didn't feel like I had another option.

Appeal to Ignorance

An appeal to ignorance fallacy occurs when an opponent makes a claim based on missing information. It is not a fallacy built around the idea that an opponent is "ignorant." For example, "My client must be innocent because no criminating e-mails exist." Does this mean that the client is innocent? Of course not. The incriminating e-mails may have been on servers that were destroyed.

Ambiguous

An argument is said to be ambiguous if there is a change in the meaning of a term or phrase within the argument or if the argument has an unclear sentence structure. For example:

> *Love* is an emotion.
> God is *love*.
> Therefore, God is an emotion.

When listening to others, we must be careful that we understand what is actually being said and what is intended. For instance, my son came home from school and announced, "We started working with clay today." Seizing an opportunity to poke a little fun, I responded, "Who's Clay?" Did he mean "clay" or "Clay?" Did I mean "Who is Clay" or "Whose clay?"

Another form of the ambiguous fallacy is called "doublespeak." Doublespeak happens when someone intentionally uses a term ambiguously. It is often employed to make an argument sound less offensive. For instance, the word "fetus" is the Latin word for an unborn child, yet abortionists prefer the term "fetus" rather than "unborn child." "Fourth trimester abortion" is a deceptive way of describing "afterbirth infanticide." "Eugenics" is a term that describes the once-legal practice in America of forced sterilization or abortions of people deemed to be inferior. Targets for the eugenics program included people with low intelligence, welfare dependents, those who were inbred, and those who were deemed to have children that they couldn't support. Today, the term "eugenics" carries a bitter taste for many Americans, so it has been replaced with the less offensive substitute, "family planning."

Beside the Point

An argument is said to be beside the point if it argues for a conclusion that is irrelevant to the immediate discussion. Rather than answering a question or address a point directly, someone might "beat around the bush" and try to switch the subject. This fallacy is often used by those who are avoiding a question that they do not wish to answer.

Black and White

The black and white fallacy typically seeks to persuade actions or opinions by insisting only one of two extreme choices is valid. Sometimes called a "false dilemma," this fallacy often includes the "either . . . or . . ." format. For example, "Either you are for equal marriage for all, or you are a bigot." The problem with this type of thinking is that it is so narrow minded that it will not allow an opponent the option to express an alternative opinion.

This tactic is tantamount to the school bully who threatens to beat up a physically weaker classmate unless he gives him his lunch money.

When the NBA cancelled its 2017 All-Star game in Charlotte, North Carolina, and the NCAA moved seven of its collegiate athletic championships out of the state, both of these organizations used the black and white fallacy. Essentially, both organizations said that either the state would have to reverse the recently enacted House Bill 2 (HB2), or they would move their events out-of-state, denying the state millions of dollars in potential revenue.

Circular

An argument is said to be circular if it presumes the truth of a conclusion, and then uses the conclusion to justify the premises. Circular arguments are frequently constructed in such a way that key words or concepts are simply redefined between the conclusion and premises. A typical circular argument looks like this:

Miracles can't happen because they are impossible.

Interestingly, Thomas Jefferson believed this and literally cut out all the miracles in his Bible, then constructed what is known as the *Jefferson Bible*, or *The Life and Morals of Jesus of Nazareth*. Regardless of Jefferson's motives, the fact remains that the statement itself is a logical fallacy. The reason this statement is a fallacy is because something that can't happen is impossible, and something that is impossible can't happen. The terms are just redefined in a circular argument.

Complex Question

A complex question is a question that assumes the truth of something that is untrue or doubtful. Typically, a complex question is a trap designed to get an opponent to admit to something that may be irrelevant to him or her. The classic question, "Are you still beating your wife?" is a complex question. To answer "no" implies that at some time in the past you did beat your wife, while a "yes" response gets you in all sorts of trouble.

False Stereotype

The false stereotype is an assumption that the members of a certain group are more alike than they really are. One effect of the false stereotype is to reduce or eliminate individuality, thereby discrediting anyone who is perceived to be a part of a particular group. "Oh you live in the rural South? You must be a guns-rights activist." "Oh, you live in California? You must be a liberal." "So, you live in Hawaii? You must be a good surfer."

Opposition Fallacy

The opposition fallacy occurs when one group is pitted against another group in such a manner that one group is always good or right and another group that is always bad or wrong. But can we ever be wrong and our opponents right instead?

I like to conduct a demonstration in my classes in which I demonstrate the foolishness of the opposition fallacy. American politics are neatly divided into the opposition fallacy. It's become commonplace for people to just leave moral decisions to their particular party representatives. They trust their representatives blindly, and quite frankly, foolishly. To conduct my demonstration, I ask, "By a show of hands, who among you would admit that you voted in the last election?" Inevitably, most students will raise a hand. Next, I ask, "Who among those of you who voted, can name the US Senators that represent you right now? Who can name your representative in the US House of Representatives? Who represents you in the state-level legislature?" If you the reader can answer these questions, you are a rare exception to the norm. Most students do not know anything about the very representatives they voted for to go make public policy decisions for them and their families. Sadly, they were duped by the opposition fallacy and remain ignorant of what is really happening in politics.

Pro–Con Fallacy

The pro–con fallacy is also called stacking the deck. In the pro–con fallacy, people will often list the weigh reasons for (pro) and against (con) an issue. The pro–con fallacy exists whenever we choose to argue in such a manner that we hide evidence that might hurt our chances of persuasion. Think of a deck of cards. You have black cards and you have red cards. The black cards represent the good arguments you can make, whereas the red cards represent the arguments your opponent can use against you. Those that use the pro–con fallacy will "stack the deck" by displaying only the black cards, or good arguments, and hiding the red cards, or bad arguments. This fallacy can be particularly deceptive.

In 2007–2008, I worked as a research associate for an organization that was involved in the debate over whether or not North Carolina should legalize gambling. To my amazement, the pro–con argument was strong enough to legalize what is now known as the North Carolina Education Lottery. Why was I amazed? Take a look at the argument that secured legalized gambling in North Carolina:

We should legalize gambling in our state because it would

bring in new tax revenue, encourage tourists to come and

spend money here, and cost nothing.

Sounds great, right? Everything appears to be true, and it seems like a compelling argument. However, let's change just one word in that argument and see how it sounds.

We should legalize prostitution *in our state because it would*

bring in new tax revenue, encourage tourists to come and

spend money here, and cost nothing.

Now, I ask, would the taxpayers still be as excited about the new tax revenue, those new tourists who come here to spend their money on prostitutes, and do they really believe such a policy will cost nothing?

Straw Man

The straw man fallacy is a clever attack which misrepresents or weakens another's position. It also occurs when someone deceptively characterizes their opposition in a false way. A typical straw man includes a positive affirmation of an opponent, followed by a false claim against the opponent. The positive affirmation builds a sense of trustworthiness which enables a lie to slip in disguised as either truth or falsehood. Someone might say, "Charles Darwin, the man that popularized the theory of Evolution, thought his grandfather was an ape." Thus the straw man in this instance began with a praise and was followed by an attack on the same character.

Key points to remember when engaging in ethical conversations

- When discussing ethics, resist the temptation to just jump in and start laying out your arguments.

- The person that makes a moral claim bears the burden of proof. What reasons does he/she have for the conclusions reached?

- Make sure you know what other people are saying. In a gentle way, get people to commit to their point.

- Anything you add to the conversation you must be prepared to defend. Be careful about what you say. Keep it simple and concentrated so you can make a solid case.

- Let others make claims and prove them. Let them explain themselves. Let them find their own logical fallacies.

- Can you justify your own views?

The people of the ancient village of Kalama in modern-day India received a lot of visitors to their town. Among them were sages, ascetics who renounced various things in life, holy people, and other persons of respect and honor. However, much like in our own day, the "wisdom" that was peddled by these passersby was contradictory. Who was right? How could they know? The people of Kalama asked the Buddha to address their concern, and his reply is recorded in the *Kalama Sutra*:

Do not believe in anything simply because you have heard it. Do not believe in traditions because they have been handed down for many generations. Do not believe in anything simply because it is spoken and rumored by many. Do not believe in anything because it is written in your religious books. Do not believe in anything merely on the authority of your teachers and elders. But after observation and analysis, when you find that anything agrees with reason and is conducive to the good and benefit of one and all, then accept it and live up to it.

—Buddha

In other words, Buddha admonished his hearers, *"Do not accept any doctrine from reverence, but first try it as gold is tried by fire."* The logical fallacies presented earlier, although but a sample of many, will help us to test the doctrines, those pillars of the mind, that we will proceed to examine.

CHAPTER 3
Moral Relativism

"In those days … everyone did what was right in his own eyes."

Judges 21:25 (NASB)

Most of us don't want someone else telling us what we should or should not do, especially when it comes to our private lives. We often hear such statements as, "Don't judge me!" or "What's good for me may not be good for you, and what's good for you may not be good for me." We insist that whatever moral choices we make are no one's business other than our own, because whatever we decide to do is right in our own eyes.

Moral relativism is the ethical theory that claims there are no moral absolutes, meaning that nothing is morally right or wrong in and of itself. Rather, rights and wrongs are based on social or even individual preferences. Essentially, moral relativism theory teaches that morality does not depend on a universal, absolute, set standard, but instead relies on generally accepted norms which can vary among nations, cultures, religions, families, and individuals. The idea of a God that gives absolute moral standards is anathema to moral relativism theory.

Moral relativism represents a break from the Greek and Hindu understandings of a preexisting rational moral order that governs the universe. Instead, relativists argue that morality is not based on any absolute, unchanging moral standards. Moral standards may change, depending on the preferences of individuals and societies. To moral relativists, democracies offer a way to express this moral idea. In a democracy, the majority opinion gets to make the rules. If you want to change the existing laws, all you need to do is to sway the majority opinion in your favor.

Moral relativism is a very tolerant ethical system. For moral relativists, no moral system is right, but none is wrong, either. Ethical systems vary from culture to culture and one person to another, and while each system has its own advantages for those who hold it, none can be proved worthy of universal acceptance. Therefore, there is no ultimate way to justify one ethical system over any other.

Jainism is a peaceful religion that traces its roots deep into ancient India. A distinguishing characteristic of Jain teachings is the relativist idea of multiple truths. Within the teachings of the Jains is the theory of Manifold Predictions, (also called *Syadvada*, or *Anekantvad*) which teaches that truth can be expressed in seven different ways. To illustrate this theory, the Jains tell the story of the blind men that meet an elephant:

Once upon a time, there lived six blind men in a village. One day the villagers told them, "Hey, there is an elephant in the village today." They had no idea what an elephant is. They decided, "Even though we would not be able to see it, let us go and feel it anyway." All of them went where the elephant was. Everyone touched the elephant. "Hey, the elephant is a pillar," said the first man who touched his leg.

"Oh no! It is like a rope," said the second man who touched the tail."

"Oh no! It is like a thick branch of a tree," said the third man who touched the trunk of the elephant.

"It is like a big hand fan," said the fourth man who touched the ear of the elephant."

"It is like a huge wall," said the fifth man who touched the belly of the elephant.

"It is like a solid pipe," said the sixth man who touched the tusk of the elephant.

They began to argue about the elephant and every one of them insisted that he was right. It looked like they were getting agitated. A wise man was passing by and he saw this. He stopped and asked them, "What is the matter?" They said, "We cannot agree to what the elephant is like." Each one of them told what he thought the elephant was like. The wise man calmly explained to them, "All of you are right. The reason every one of you is telling it differently is because each one of you touched a different part of the elephant. So, actually the elephant has all those features what you all said."

"Oh!" everyone said. There was no more fight. They felt happy that they were all right.

–Ancient Indian Fable, Public Domain

The moral of this story is that truth is relative, and because truth is relative, we should respect the opinions of others. After all, their view of reality is based on a different perspective than our own.

To moral relativists, what is considered good today may be considered evil tomorrow, and what is considered evil today may be considered good tomorrow. Right and wrong, good and evil, justice and injustice, are relegated to mere opinions.

TYPES OF MORAL RELATIVISM

Objectivism is the view that some moral principles apply to everyone. To claim honor killings is morally wrong—no matter where it's done or who does it is a morally objective statement.

Ethical relativism is the position that there are no moral absolutes; nor moral rights and wrongs. Rights and wrongs are based on social norms.

Cultural relativism is the view that an action is morally right if one's culture approves of it. A 32 percent conviction rate for 8,233 dowry-related murders seems to indicate that a significant portion of the Indian population condones this practice.

Subjective relativism is the view that an action is morally right if one approves it. This position implies that it is futile to argue that someone is morally wrong.

Moral infallibility refers to the idea that for each and any moral opinion, each person is incapable of being in error. If we sincerely approve of an action, then that action is morally right. Thus, when we say an action is right, we are just saying that we approve of it. When we say an action is wrong, we are just saying that we disapprove of it.

Emotivism is the view that moral utterances are neither true nor false but are expressions of emotions or attitudes. It implies that people cannot disagree over the moral facts because there are no moral facts, and that presenting reasons in support of a moral utterance is a matter of offering nonmoral facts that can influence someone's attitude, and that nothing is actually good or bad.

Epicureanism is a school of philosophy begun by Epicurus (341–270 BC) which taught that there are many gods, but those gods do not immanently interfere with human affairs. Because these gods are transcendent above, but not immanent with the material world, mankind is free to exercise the freedom to pursue pleasures without fear of judgment in a nonexistent afterlife for living an "immoral" life. The idea of sin is simply not plausible.

To Epicureans, life—indeed reality itself—is just a mechanical outworking of atoms and empty space. Thus, life is meaningless apart from deriving pleasure. In fact, pleasure is the greatest good, and suffering and other pains are the greatest evils. Further, all people have free will and should use that free will to pursue pleasures and avoid displeasures. After all, life ceases at death, so there is no moral judgment to follow in a nonexistent afterlife.

ADVOCATES OF MORAL RELATIVISM

Protagoras (c.490/481–420 BC) is considered by many to be the "Father of Relativism," as well as the "Father of Agnosticism." Born in Abdera in Thrace, Protagoras is the most well-known of the Sophist philosophers. These terms are fitting, although a bit misleading. They are fitting in that relativism and agnosticism are closely related, and that moral relativism and agnosticism are both very old ideas. However, they are misleading in that both relativism and agnosticism are indeed much older than Protagoras.

Of his writings, we only know of two: *Alethia*, or *Truth*, and *Peritheon*, or *On the Gods. Alethia* is Protagoras' attempt to explain truth, and in it he writes, "Man is the measure of all things: of things which are, that they are, and of things which are not, that they are not."

Most of what we know about Protagoras comes from Plato's *Theaetetus* and *Protagoras*. In *Theaetetus*, Plato presents Protagoras as saying that ethical practices are relative to the State: "For I hold that whatever practices seem right and laudable to any particular State are so for that State, so long as it holds by them." Yet in *Protagoras*, he is presented as holding a view in which the individual is held accountable for ethical norms since these norms are given by the gods: "because few cities could not exist if, as in the case of other arts, few men only were partakers of them."

Just how does Protagoras warrant the title, *Father of Agnosticism*, if he believes that moral norms are given by the gods? He writes, "With regards to the gods, I cannot feel sure either that they are or that they are not, nor what they are like in figure; for there are many things that hinder sure knowledge, the obscurity of the subject and the shortness of human life."

Thus, Protagoras would seem to suggest that while we cannot know certain things about the gods, we can abide by the laws, traditions, and customs handed down in our culture, as these reflect the moral will of the gods for mankind, which in turn is generally agreed upon by the individuals of that culture.

Therefore, we must ask ourselves, "Is morality determined by the State, or does mankind ultimately know deeply within himself what is morally right or wrong?"

Heraclitus (535–475 BC) derives one of his most famous observations about morality from along the banks of a river. He writes, *"On those stepping into rivers staying the same other and other waters flow."*

The point Heraclitus makes is that he believed nothing is stable, but everything is always in a state of flux, or change. For instance, there is no "same river," as the water that constitutes a river at a particular moment in time is in a constant state of motion. Therefore, he concludes that perhaps good and evil change also, meaning that something considered good today could be considered evil tomorrow and something considered evil today could be considered good tomorrow.

Friedrich Nietzsche (1844–1900) was the epitome of the prodigal child. Although his grandfather and his father were both Lutheran theologians, Friedrich Nietzsche made his mark on the world, not by upholding morality, but by a "campaign against morality."

Nietzsche wrote many works including: *Thus Spoke Zarathustra, The Will to Power, Towards a Genealogy of Morals,* and *Beyond Good and Evil.*

The influence of Darwin's theory of evolution is clear in the writings of Nietzsche. However, we must be aware of the distinction between Darwin's mere survival of the fittest and Nietzsche's ideal "will to power." The "fittest" man for Nietzsche aims not for mere survival, but to dominate. Nietzsche despised what he perceived as the weakness of Judeo-Christian values such as humility, sympathy, and love for one's neighbors. Rather, Nietzsche exalted the counter values such as pride, contempt, and lack of tolerance. To him, the fittest man, or the "Superman" is one who determines his own values and lives by his own set of rules. Thus, Nietzsche's "superman" is nothing less than a man-made god himself.

OPPONENTS OF MORAL RELATIVISM

Plato (c.428/427–348/347 BC) was a Greek aristocratic philosopher and founder of the Academy of Athens, the first school for higher learning in the Western world. Plato himself was a student of Socrates, and Plato later became the teacher of Aristotle. So great has been Plato's influence in philosophy that Albert North Whitehead writes, *"The safest general characterization of the European philosophical tradition is that it consists of a series of footnotes to Plato."*[1]

Plato questioned Heraclitus' reasoning about everything being a state of flux. Does this mean that knowledge is constantly changing, too? To Plato, who believed that there was an invisible world of unchanging absolutes that allows us to know anything at all, this idea was ridiculous.

Stoic Philosophy was founded by Zeno of Citium around 300 BC. Stoic philosophy views the world as being permeated by a rational soul and divinely organized into a perfect harmony or unity. The wisest possible way to live is to live according to this cosmic unity. If one can cultivate this harmony in life, then he can discover his place in the overall grand scheme of the cosmos.

Stoic philosophy is at odds with moral relativism on several key fronts. Two of those involve the idea of responsibility toward others and the concept of vices and virtues.

---

[1] Alfred North Whitehead, *Process and Reality* (New York: Free Press, 1979), 39.

As a part of the cosmic unity, the Stoics maintained that to live in harmony and experience peace and happiness, one must live in harmony with those around him.

In regard to virtues and vices, Stoics acknowledged that virtues are an integral part of wise living, whereas vices, or ruling passions of foolishness, destroy peace and happiness and cause one to live apart from harmony with others and the cosmos.

Critique of Moral Relativism

Genuine disagreement about moral issues is a fact in the world. Does this mean that nothing in and of itself is *just wrong*? Consider the stories below:

Female Genital Mutilation

Female genital mutilation (FGM) involves removing all or part of the female genitals. In Africa, the Middle East, and parts of Asia, FGM is practiced on girls from infancy to 15, but older girls also may have the procedure.

FGM is done for religious and sociological reasons. Some say it prepares girls for their role in society and marriage and discourages illicit sex.

Those who oppose the practice argue that FGM is a serious health problem. The World Health Organization reports that FGM exposes girls to reproductive tract infections, pain during intercourse, painful menstruation, complications during childbirth, hemorrhaging, and even death. http://www.who.int/mediacentre/factsheets/fs241/en/

Do you think FGC is morally permissible even if it is approved in those cultures? Why or why not?

Family Honor Killings

In Pakistan, a young woman and her fiancé were met at a local courthouse by the bride-to-be's nonconsenting family. Citing religious differences, the woman's family killed her with bricks from a nearby construction site. Should we be alarmed at the practice of honor killings, or should we just accept it as a cultural difference and ignore it? What happens if those who practice honor killings migrate to other areas of the world that don't condone such actions?

SEXUAL ETHICS

Sexual ethics is a particularly controversial topic today. How much freedom should society allow others to express themselves sexually? Should anything and everything be permissible as long as it occurs among consenting adults? What about consenting persons that may not be adults? Can you think of any sexual practice that should be considered morally taboo? By which moral authority do you make your claim?

Incest

In 2016, a 43-year-old Oklahoma mother and her 25-year-old daughter were arrested and jailed under $10,000 bail for being married to each other. Records show that the mother had previously been married to her son, but that marriage was annulled 15 months later in 2010.

Also in 2016, a 36-year-old New Mexico mother and 19-year-old son were arrested for being in an incestuous relationship after admitting they were sexually involved to police investigators.

If morality is truly relative and dependent on the individuals involved, then shouldn't laws against incest be considered bad laws that need to be overturned?

Bestiality

On Monday, September16, 2013, the Fayetteville (North Carolina) Observer published a story titled, "Police Accuse Ft. Bragg Soldier and His Wife of Making Pornography with Dogs." They were charged with multiple counts of crimes against nature involving bestiality, disseminating obscene materials, and conspiracy, and bail for each was set at $15,000. A similar story was released in the summer of 2016 in which a Georgia man was observed having sex with a female goat. He was arrested and released on $1,300 bond. Were any of these individuals acting immorally by simply practicing bestiality? Why or why not?

Pedophilia

In 2013 an 8-year-old girl died from internal injuries on her wedding night in Yemen. The injuries occurred during consummation of her arranged marriage to a 40-year-old man. A combination of tribal tradition and religious permission means that this form of pedophilia will continue.

Most people in America still generally believe that pedophilia is a particularly heinous act. Often, adults found guilty of pedophilia are sent to prison. Can we say that pedophilia is always wrong though? What if it occurs between consenting couples of various ages? Is it wrong to discriminate based on age differences? Could we, like the blind men describing the elephant, be wrongfully considering pedophilia from our own biased perspective? How would you justify your own opinions regarding sexual ethics?

Moral Relativism and the French Revolution

As we can see, unbridled moral relativism can have a dark side. The French Bohemians, a group of followers of Rousseau's philosophy of absolute freedom from any and all social and moral constraints, wanted their complete freedom so badly they initiated the French Revolution. Robespierre, known for his "Reign of Terror," rose to power and aided their cause by silencing their opposition with the guillotine. Thousands who dared to express their moral concerns were beheaded, while countless others remained silent just to preserve their own lives.

Today, while the guillotine itself isn't being used to ensure the silence of opposition to complete moral freedom, heads are being figuratively chopped off as lives and careers are ruined by carefully-crafted news stories, special-interest activists on social media, and in some courts.

"Once a government is committed to the principle of silencing the voice of opposition, it has only one way to go, and that is down the path of increasingly repressive measures, until it becomes a source of terror to all its citizens and creates a country where everyone lives in fear."

—President Harry S. Truman

CONCLUDING REMARKS ABOUT MORAL RELATIVISM

Moral relativism is a popular belief today for various reasons, but it should be challenged with more scrutiny. For instance, why might someone feel that incest is wrong? Or that bestiality is repulsive? Or that an adult involved in a pedophiliac relationship with a consenting teenager should be imprisoned? These acts are, after all, considered taboo by society, but we must ask ourselves, "Why are these acts considered taboo?" There is clearly a majority within society that generally feels that such acts are "just wrong"; otherwise these acts would not produce such feelings of angst inside of us.

Next, we must contend with the idea that we are a democracy since this misguided opinion has been popularized in recent generations. A democracy is a form of government in which the majority opinion determines what is right or wrong for society. When society rejects the moral status quo, they can appeal to have laws changed. Like Heraclitus' observation of the river being always in a state of flux, in a democracy, morality is always in a state of flux. Thus, a democracy would seem to be an ideal system of government for those who espouse moral relativism.

We will formally explore the philosophical principles of a democracy later. But in the meantime, how is it that the will of the voting majority of the population is sometimes upheld and sometimes denied? Moreover, would we still feel the same way about a democracy, or more specifically the "rightness" of cultural norms if the majority wanted to reinstill slave-ownership laws? Is the majority opinion ever wrong, and should the majority really determine what is right or wrong for the minority?

Today, much of the Western world denies the concept of a divine Creator and moral Lawgiver. Without such a Being, there is no rational order to the world, and certainly no wise, absolute moral order. Just as the universe, humanity, and everything else exists by random chance, so our morality is also random and irrational. After all, there is no absolute standard for morality. Therefore, moral relativism insists that the best way to live is to ignore reason.

Is this really the wisest way to live? Does something inside of you tell you that it is just wrong to set your sister-in-law on fire because the dowry amount was inadequate or because her family has been too slow to pay? Is there something inside of you that says that it is just wrong for humans to have sex with animals, or for adults to have sex with children? Perhaps something inside of you says that it is wrong for a mother to marry her children. Lots of people feel a degree of angst over "gender fluidity," in which a person claims to switch genders. Does this angst have a legitimate rational basis grounded in rational wisdom, or should it be ignored? We must remember that the wisest teachers the world has ever known proclaim that the key to living a wise life is to seek wisdom, not ignore it.

SHARPENING YOUR OWN CRITICAL THINKING SKILLS

1. Describe the concept of "moral relativism".
2. Explain how the historical development of moral relativism has impacted Western culture today.
3. List three benefits of moral relativism.
4. List three problems with moral relativism.
5. What would you think might happen if society adopted Rousseau's belief that people should be completely free from any and all moral constraints and live by their own moral code of ethics?
6. What are "moral absolutes"? Do you believe there are any moral absolutes? Why or why not? Are you absolutely sure?
7. Heraclitus believed that all knowledge is in flux, and therefore all knowledge is based on interpretation rather than objective truth. What was Plato's response to Herodotus concerning this? What is your own response to Heraclitus and Plato?
8. What is moral relativism's fundamental influence on a democracy?

CHAPTER 4
Egoism

Egoism is the very essence of a noble soul.

—Friedrich Nietzsche

Of all the degrading vices egoism is the most vile and despicable one.

—William Thackeray

TERMS

Ethical egoism is the moral theory that says men ought to act in their own self-interest. We each have one life to live, therefore we should maximize our own happiness in this life. James Rachels says, "ethical egoism is the idea that people have moral obligations only to themselves and that they ought to pursue their own ends exclusively." An ethical egoist would argue that people should be selfish and would say that one has no duty whatsoever to help anyone else in need unless by doing so one's own needs would be met.

Some ethical egoists argue that is always moral to act in one's own interest and it is always immoral to not act in one's own self-interest. This view is known as the strong view of ethical egoism. The weak view of ethical egoism also maintains that it is always moral to act in one's own interest, but it allows for instances in which personal interest is not the chief aim of an action.

Psychological egoism is the perceived observation that all men act selfishly all the time. The only motive that moves men to act is selfishness.

Rational egoism is the moral theory that it is rational to look out for your own interests. Ayn Rand is perhaps the most famous proponent of rational egoism.

Conditional egoism is the moral theory that is concerned with the end result of an action. According to this theory, man is justified in his selfishness as long as his selfishness contributes to the good of society. One of the chief weaknesses with conditional egoism is that it struggles to explain who determines the public good.

Unlike egoism, **altruism** is a competing moral theory that says man ought not be selfish but instead should be helpful to others. The Golden Rule, "treat others as you would want them to treat you" is an altruistic statement.

Heartland Arts/Shutterstock.com

Adam Smith

Adam Smith (1723–1790) was a Scottish entrepreneur, lecturer, and philosopher who advocated a form of egoism which incorporated altruism. Dubbed the "Adam Smith problem," this was in essence a conditional egoism in which Smith recognized that people tend to work naturally to the benefit of their own self-interest, but wherein one's self-interest was also acknowledged to be interwoven with the self-interest of others. Thus, Smith argues that self-interest is maximized in an economy in which man is free from government restraint and allowed to maximize his own talents.

In 1776, Smith published *An Enquiry into the Nature and Causes of the Wealth of Nations* in which he argued that entrepreneurs should have freedom to promote their own business interests by developing their own talents and maximizing their profits, because the by-product of such actions would include benefits to the surrounding community. He writes,

> It is not from the benevolence of the butcher, the brewer, or the baker that we expect our dinner, but from their regard to their own interest . . . In a tribe of hunters or shepherds a particular person makes bows and arrows, for example, with more readiness and dexterity than any other. He frequently exchanges them for cattle or for venison with his companions; and he finds at last that he can in this manner get more cattle and venison than if he himself went to the field to catch them. From a regard to his own interest, therefore, the making of bows and arrows grows to be his chief business, and he becomes a sort of armourer. Another excels in making the frames and covers of their little huts or movable houses. He is accustomed to be of use in this way to his neighbors, who reward him in the same manner with cattle and venison, till at last he finds it his interest to dedicate himself entirely to this employment, and to become a sort of house-carpenter. In the same manner a third becomes

a smith or a brazier, a fourth a tanner . . . And thus the certainty of being able to exchange all that surplus part of the produce of his own labour, which is over and above his own consumption, for such parts of the produce of other men's labour as he may have occasion for, encourages every man to apply himself to a particular occupation, and to cultivate and bring to perfection whatever talent or genius he may possess for that particular species of business.

—Adam Smith, *Wealth of Nations*, Book 1, Chapter 2

Smith's point is that the freedom to maximize our talents enables us to market our labor, and to rightfully receive a just reward for our efforts. The reward we receive is in relation to the demand for the fruit of our labor. If one is prosperous and has acquired an element of wealth then the wealth can be used to barter for the fruit of another's labor.

Ayn Rand (1905 – 1982)

At the age of nine, Ayn Rand decided she wanted to become a professional fiction writer. Her determination paid off as her published works include *Anthem*, *The Fountainhead*, and *Atlas Shrugged*. After being rejected by twelve publishers, *The Fountainhead* became a bestseller in 1945. Her most famous work, however, was *Atlas Shrugged* which was published in 1957.

As a teenager in Russia, Rand witnessed both the Kerensky Revolution and the Bolshevik Revolution. Her family fled to the Crimea to escape the fighting and while in high school there, she studied American history and became enamored with American freedom. In February 1926, Rand arrived in New York City and spent the next six months living with relatives in Chicago. Next, she went to Hollywood to try to lend a career as a screenwriter. On her second day there, she met her husband of 50 years, an actor named Frank O'Connor.

We include Ayn Rand in the category of egoism because of her emphasis on the self. As a self-described rational egoist, we could just as easily place her in the category of reason because of her emphasis on the mind's ability to rationalize, which she believes leads to the good that follows correct reasoning.

I am not primarily an advocate of capitalism, but of egoism;

I am not primarily an advocate of egoism, but of reason.

If one recognizes the supremacy of reason and
applies it consistently, all the rest follows.

—Ayn Rand

Rand officially calls her philosophy "objectivism." **Objectivism** maintains that reality consists of facts, which are absolute truths that are not up for debate. **Subjectivism**, on the other hand, maintains that truth and reality are constructs of one's mind, or to put it another way, the product of mental operations. Thus, a subjectivist may wish to hold a different opinion from established facts, but an objectivist rejects such a position on the grounds that the denial of established truths is foolish and unreasonable.

Like Friedrich Nietzsche, whom we will study in more detail later, Rand is concerned with the development of the full potential of self and they both passionately believe that religious institutions are to blame for stifling the full development of mankind. To both Nietzsche and Rand, the moral code of egoism is the only standard of moral conduct that can bring this about. Interestingly, when we study humanism we will find that humanists are also concerned about the full development of mankind; however, humanists reject Rand's egoism in favor of a more encompassing utilitarianism.

In *Atlas Shrugged*, Rand includes a fictional character named John Galt who was working at a motor factory that decided to implement a socialist form of government. A form of utilitarianism, the socialist system meant that workers were paid according to their need—not according to their ability. Lower-skilled workers were paid the same as higher-skilled workers. The result was a form of wealth redistribution that discouraged workers from being independent and creative. Realizing that this was not a fair system, workers exaggerated or faked their need to retain more wealth. John Galt disagreed with the newly implemented socialist system and left the company because wanted to enjoy the fruits of his own labor and be rewarded for his own talents. As he was leaving, he vowed "to shut down the motor of the world."

Critics of Ayn Rand note that she is particularly opposed to altruism. In a 1959 television interview with Mike Wallace, Rand claims that altruism is evil, because in her mind, altruism makes man a sacrificial animal. Rand argued that man should not neglect his own self; in fact, his moral priority should be to himself, and that he alone is responsible for his own happiness.

My philosophy, in essence, is the concept of man as a heroic being, with his own happiness as the moral purpose of his life, with productive achievement as his noblest activity, and reason as his only absolute.

—Ayn Rand

The Golden Rule

The primary teaching of every religion?

Christianity: In everything, do to others as you would have them do to you; for this is the law and the prophets. (Jesus, Matthew 7:12)

Sikhism: I am a stranger to no one; and no one is a stranger to me. Indeed, I am a friend to all. (Guru Granth Sahib, p. 1299)

Islam: Not one of you truly believes until you wish for others what you wish for yourself. (The Prophet Muhammad, Hadith)

Zoroastrianism: Do not do unto others whatever is injurious to yourself. (Shayast-na-Shayast 13.29)

Hinduism: This is the sum of duty: do not do to others what would cause pain if done to you. (Mahabharata 5:1517)

Buddhism: Treat not others in ways that you yourself would find hurtful. (Udana-Varga 5.18)

Judaism: What is hateful to you, do not do to your neighbour. This is the whole Torah; all the rest is commentary. (Hillel, Talmud, Shabbat 31a)``

Jainism: One should treat all creatures in the world as one would like to be treated. (Mahavira, Sutrakritanga)

Taoism: Regard your neighbour's gain as your own gain, and your neighbour's loss as your own loss. (T'ai Shang Kan Ying P'ien, 213–218)

Practically, we find not only that Rand rejects the Golden Rule and the religious institutions that advocated this rule, but ironically, her egoism is borrowed from a core religious principle known as the parable of the talents:

Again, it will be like a man going on a journey, who called his servants and entrusted his wealth to them. To one he gave five bags of gold, to another two bags, and to another one bag, each according to his ability. Then he went on his journey. The man who had received five bags of gold went at once and put his money to work and gained five bags more. So also, the one with two bags of gold gained two more. But the man who had received one bag went off, dug a hole in the ground and hid his master's money. After a long time the master of those servants returned and settled accounts with them. The man who had received five bags of gold brought the other five. 'Master,' he said, 'you entrusted me with five bags of gold. See, I have gained five more.' His master replied, 'Well done, good and faithful servant! You have been faithful with a few things; I will put you in charge of many things. Come and share your master's happiness!' The man with two bags of gold also came. 'Master,' he said, 'you entrusted me with two bags of gold; see, I have gained two more.' His master replied, 'Well done, good and faithful servant! You have been faithful with a few things; I will put you in charge of many things.

Come and share your master's happiness!' Then the man who had received one bag of gold came. 'Master,' he said, 'I knew that you are a hard man, harvesting where you have not sown and gathering where you have not scattered seed. So I was afraid and went out and hid your gold in the ground. See, here is what belongs to you.' His master replied, 'You wicked, lazy servant! So you knew that I harvest where I have not sown and gather where I have not scattered seed? Well then, you should have put my money on deposit with the bankers, so that when I returned I would have received it back with interest. 'So take the bag of gold from him and give it to the one who has ten bags. For whoever has will be given more, and they will have an abundance. Whoever does not have, even what they have will be taken from them. And throw that worthless servant outside, into the darkness, where there will be weeping and gnashing of teeth.'

—Matthew 25:14–30 (NIV)

Georgios Kollidas/Shutterstock.com

Thomas Hobbes (1588–1679)

At one time, Thomas Hobbes was categorized as an egoist, because his theory of the psychology of human nature insists that people are completely and exclusively egotistic. He thinks people are completely selfish and empty of any genuine feelings of sympathy, benevolence, or sociability. An understanding of his thought processes will enable us to better understand the roots of egoism.

Hobbes lived during the late Renaissance and was an early contemporary with the Enlightenment. Both the Renaissance and the Enlightenment provided tremendous advancements in science each marks a dramatic shift in the way people view the world. When Magellan set out to sail around the world he didn't fall off. Using a telescope, Galileo observed that the earth revolved around the sun, which disproved the prevailing theory that the Earth was the center of the universe. Microscopes enabled people to discover and observe cells. Isaac Newton discovered the law of gravity, developed three laws of motion, discovered calculus, and he also discovered the color spectrum while studying white light. People were literally looking at the world in a way they had never done before. Renaissance art is characterized by depth and landscapes which captured the inquisitive nature of the time. People began to question the knowledge of the world, and the authorities which gave them that knowledge. The educated class at the time consisted of the rulers and the clergy. These were the dispensers of knowledge and they had been proven wrong. Thus, people wondered what else were they being misled about. This gave rise to a loosening of theological convictions as people increasingly questioned the authority of the religious texts.

Such was the context in which Thomas Hobbes lived. Hobbes believed the laws of science apply to human nature. He believed that the body and mind are of the same substances, and that mental actions are nothing but physiological motions. Hobbes describes voluntary actions as a variety of animal emotions, which he calls endeavors. These he defined as predispositions to act in a certain direction. For example, when you get hungry you go eat. When you get thirsty, you go get something to drink. We don't have to be told to breathe.

Hobbes believed endeavors are mechanically initiated by sense experiences, which are supplemented by the action of imagination and memory, and determined by a calculated appraisal of the situation.

To illustrate, imagine a pair of kids walking through the woods one day, when they stumble upon a strange, large, gray, bag-like mass hanging from a tree branch. "What is it?" they ask. They don't know, so they decide to knock it out of the tree to take a better look. As they pelt the thing, a swarm of hornets descend from the bottom and proceed to sting them as they run away. The next year, the same pair of kids go walking through the woods and they stumble upon a familiar, large, gray, bag-like mass hanging from a tree branch. This time they know what it is and they decide to leave it alone. Why would they make that decision? This reiterates Hobbes' point: the kids remembered what happened the last time they encountered the large, gray, bag-like mass hanging from a tree branch and they did not want to repeat the experience.

Hobbes believed the most important kinds of endeavors are desires and aversions. Desires move one to pursue objects, and aversions move one to avoid objects. Further, endeavors are not only the chief determinants of behavior, but also the basis of evaluations and moral interpretations.

To Hobbes, evaluating objects or actions as good or evil depends solely on desires and aversions. No objects or actions are intrinsically good. Rather, good is defined by the object of our desires and evil are the objects of our aversions.

What we find is that, according to Hobbes, the same object can be simultaneously good, neutral, and evil. Values become relative to individuals. What is good for you may not necessarily be good for me and vice versa. Therefore, there is no absolute standard for morality, and if there is no absolute standard for morality then why should I not be selfish and do what I want to do? While this is an appealing idea for egoists and moral relativist alike, we have to ask ourselves, is this a reasonable theory?

A critical problem with Hobbes' theory is that it violates Aristotle's law of noncontradiction. The law of noncontradiction states, "something cannot be A and non-A at the same time." This means someone cannot be pregnant and nonpregnant at the same time. Someone cannot be employed and unemployed at the same time. Likewise, something cannot be "good" and "evil" at the same time, for evil is the negation of good.

1. How might both Smith's and Rand's assessment that people should be free to maximize their talents actually be considered somewhat altruistic?

2. Why does Ayn Rand reject the Golden rule?

3. Do you agree or disagree with Hobbes that people are always selfish? Can you think of anyone who is not always selfish?

4. Can you think of any moral actions that invalidate Hobbes' theory by violating Aristotle's law of noncontradiction? If so, list them.

5. How are Plato's quest for the understanding of the "Good" and Nietzsche's quest for truth related?

6. Why do both Nietzsche and Rand reject religious authority?

7. In what ways did the Renaissance period affect people's perspective of reality?

8. What is the difference between objectivism and subjectivism?

9. How is the Parable of the Talents different than the socialism that Ayn Rand objects to in her novel, *Atlas Shrugged*?

10. In what way does Thomas Hobbes appear to accept subjectivism?

CHAPTER 5
Value

One of the most challenging questions in moral philosophy is: What is the good life? What makes the question so difficult to negotiate is that the answer depends on determining just what things are valuable to desire, to pursue, and to have. The complexity in this is immediately apparent when we consider the myriad desires persons have and the multitude of things we believe have some sort of value in our lives. We have interests and desires and tend to think that whatever satisfies those is good for us in that it makes a positive difference to us. We believe that some things have negative value or are bad for us; they make a difference to us, but not in a positive way. We also tend to think that something has positive value for us when it aids in our getting something else. For instance, going to college is good because it is a way to earn a degree, having a degree is a means to a good job, having a good job leads to making money, having money is a way to get other things—a nice car, a home theatre, a trip to Italy, membership in an upscale golf club, and so on. But is everything we call good or valuable good in this sense? Is everything good only in so far as it delivers something else that makes a positive difference to us? Can we persist in the line of thinking that views all goods as means to something else? Wouldn't we arrive at a stopping place? Why might you want the nice car, the home theatre, the trip to Italy, the golf club membership? A typical answer goes something like this: It would make me happy to have and do those things.

Now consider: Does it make sense, in this case, to ask why do you want to be happy? Here we may have reached the end of the line in our questioning, not because happiness itself isn't good, but precisely because it is good, but in a special way—good not as means to something else, but good as an end in itself, as that which might have been the ultimate goal all along. Is there an ultimate good for us? Is that good happiness or something else? If there is something that is of ultimate value for us, then it must matter with respect to what it means to lead a good life. The question of what, if anything, has ultimate value for us involves a nexus of concerns about having certain kinds of conscious states, performing actions, the evaluation of desires and preferences, what sorts of things are worth wanting, the pursuit of objectively determinable goods, and the communal context in which we seek satisfaction and pursue our goals. In fine, the idea of value is central to our understanding of what it means to live a life that is worth living.

The idea of the good life is, of course, an age-old problem, but there are contemporary exigencies that make it perhaps more pressing now than ever that we treat the problem with a renewed sense of importance. Peter Singer, the contemporary moral philosopher, writes that there is a "need to challenge the dominance of the assumption that the good life requires ever-rising standards of moral material affluence" as there seems to be no evidence that material wealth makes persons happier. In addition, he suggests that the current affluent lifestyle of many persons strains our planet's resources and limits its capacity to accommodate all the waste such a lifestyle produces.[1] If one thinks of the good life as inextricably connected to our being global citizens, then this view might appear especially significant. Or consider a different line of thought, one more closely associated with the idea that the good life requires living a life of self-determination, relatively free from external constraints and reasonably free to live as one chooses without fear of harm or annihilation. Many people in the contemporary world live under the oppression of unjust political power or the fear of fanaticism and are unable to live their lives as they desire. If one thinks that oppression, fanaticism, terror, and torture threaten the very possibility of achieving good ends, then that may be the prompt for deeper reflection and a revived sense of urgency about the importance of value and goodness in human life. The point here is not that we must decide which of these views is correct, but rather that the problem of the good life is not merely an abstract consideration. The concrete realities of life may alter our conception of what counts as good but not our idea that the good matters at all.

The question here is really one about means to ends. If we can identify the good, then we should be able to figure out how best to achieve it. There are two different senses of the term good then that are applicable here. Something can be good as a means to an end, or something can be good as an end or that which we hope to achieve. That which is good as a means is called an *instrumental good*. Think again about the examples above. We value money, for instance. It is a good for us, but it is not an end in itself. We use it for getting other things that we might deem valuable. That which is good in itself is called an *intrinsic good*. An intrinsic good is something that is worth having on its own; we don't use it for something else the way we use money to purchase things. Instead the intrinsic good is understood as that which is valuable to have for no other purpose than that it is good for us. This is an impor-tant distinction because it implies that there must be something that constitutes an ultimate good; that is, something is good as a means to an end only if the end is something that is itself good. If there was no good or desirable end, then it wouldn't make sense to speak of something good as means to that end. To say otherwise would involve us in an infinite regress: A is good because it is a means to B; B is good because it is a means to C; C is good because it is a means to D; and so on *ad infinitum*. So there needs to be a stopping place, without which there would be an infinite set of goods with no distinct reason as to why any of them are good at all. So the problem of the good is not fundamentally about this or that thing in a series of goods, but about what gives meaning to the whole series itself. We can say it's about what makes it all worthwhile.

Though we speak of something's being intrinsically good or having value in and of itself, it is nonetheless the case that even that which is good in itself has worth *for* us. Something has value or worth *for* us because we are conscious creatures. Consciousness is the condition for experiencing the good and being aware of its worth. Desire itself is a conscious state that directs us toward that which we find desirable. In this regard, there is nothing that is good for a rock or any inanimate object. But there are many living things that also lack consciousness. Take a plant, for instance. We do often say that it is good for a houseplant to have the proper amount of water and light in order to thrive. All we really mean here is that the plant has a biological need for sufficient water and light if it is to continue to survive; it makes no sense to say that the plant "desires" water and light, that it "finds" water and light valuable, or that it "judges" its life worthwhile if it has those things. Matters get more complicated when we think of animals, especially higher order animals that do display a degree of consciousness, which may minimally require that we treat them with a certain measure of moral respect, if not accord them some capacity to pursue desired ends. The general point here is that the good is only good for a thing if that thing has the ability to experience it.

It is one thing, however, to say that consciousness is the condition for something being good for us and quite another to say that the good itself is a state of consciousness; pleasure, for instance. Many philosophers argue that only states of consciousness—pleasant feelings or pleasurable sensations perhaps—can qualify as intrinsically good. Others argue that it is not the state of consciousness itself that matters but rather suggest that the kind of object that is desired is what matters to us. One way of considering this difference is to ask the following question: Is the good simply having certain experiences or is it experiencing things of a certain sort and in a certain way? There is a difference, for instance, in being able to play the guitar and having a pleasant experience in doing so. Do we only want to feel good or do we desire to do things and perform actions? Is the good realized in the experience alone or in the performance or ability itself? Such questions lead us squarely to a consideration of competing philosophical theories about the nature of the good.

HEDONISM

One particularly enduring conception of the good is that given in a theory called hedonism. Hedonism is rooted in a view of human nature and human psychology that says we are fundamentally motivated to experience pleasure and avoid pain. Under this view, pleasure is desired as an end and pain is considered to be that which is undesirable. The hedonist argues that:

1. Something is good if and only if it is desirable as an end in itself.
2. Only pleasure is desirable as an end in itself.
3. Therefore, only pleasure is good.

Hedonism relies on the distinction drawn above between intrinsic and instrumental goods, and makes two fundamental claims: 1) all pleasure is intrinsically good and 2) only pleasure is intrinsically good. Of course, there are many things that are instrumentally good insofar as they bring about pleasure. For example, liberty is an instrumental good as a means to experiencing more and greater pleasure. It might even be the case that although pain is in and of itself something undesirable, it can be instrumental for experiencing pleasure. Think of the physical pain you may experience as the result of a vigorous workout and the pleasure felt as a result of an improved bodily condition. It is the pleasure that we are ultimately after and we are perhaps even willing to endure a bit of pain to get there.

Now we can understand hedonism more fully. The hedonist believes that the only thing that is desirable in itself is pleasure. Pleasure is the only thing that we desire for its own sake, and not because it leads to something else that is desirable. In saying that pleasure is the only thing that is desirable in itself, hedonism is not saying that one's own pleasure counts more than anyone else's experience. Hedonism is not the same thing as egoism. In contrast to egoism, hedonists claim that anyone's pleasure is good. It doesn't matter whether it's mine or yours; pleasure, all pleasure, is good.

This form of hedonism serves as the foundation for the development of the normative ethical theory called *utilitarianism*. Utilitarianism is a type of theory called *consequentialism*. Consequentialism is the idea that the rightness or wrongness of an action is determined by the consequences, good or bad respectively, of the action. The distinguishing feature of utilitarianism is that it holds that we should perform those actions which maximize good consequences, not just for ourselves but ideally for all those who are affected by the action; that is, we should strive to bring about "the greatest good for the greatest number."

The early utilitarian thinkers Jeremy Bentham (1748–1832) and John Stuart Mill (1806–1873) were hedonists in that they identified pleasure as the greatest good. They understood the utility of an action as its tendency to increase pleasure and diminish pain. Under this view, an action has positive utility if brings about more pleasure than pain and negative utility if it does the opposite. Actions thus have instrumental value in that they are the means for securing the good. Utilitarianism views morality as an effort to ensure that as many as possible are able to experience the good to some extent or other. The next chapter focuses on utilitarianism as a normative moral theory; here the emphasis is on the idea of the good itself as that which motivates moral action.

Though both Bentham and Mill are hedonists, their views differ in significant ways, specifically with respect to both the sources of pleasure and kinds of pleasures. The Benthamite view is a *quantitative* form of hedonism. For Bentham, all pleasures are equal as being goods in themselves; pleasures differ only in amount or degrees of magnitude. There is no difference among the sources of pleasure as they are evaluated solely in terms of their capacity to produce the greatest amount of pleasure. There would be no difference between playing a simple game and listening to music or reading poetry. Bentham writes:

> ... the value they possess is exactly in proportion to the pleasure they yield.... Prejudice apart, the game of push-pin is of equal value with the arts and sciences of music and poetry. If the game of push-pin furnish more pleasure, it is more valuable than either. Everybody can play at push-pin: poetry and music are relished only by a few.... If poetry and music deserve to be preferred before a game of push-pin, it must be because they are **calculated** [my emphasis] to gratify those individuals who are most difficult to be pleased.[2]

The idea of calculated gratification is emphasized here because Bentham designed a set of quasi-mathematical criteria—the hedonistic calculus, as it is often called—to measure magnitudes of and relationships among pleasurable states as well as the tendency of acts to produce those states. Bentham considered pleasure or pain as a straightforward bodily sensation and believed that such a sensation could be measured according to the following standards:

1. *intensity,*
2. *duration,*
3. *certainty,*
4. *propinquity,*
5. *fecundity,*
6. *purity,* and
7. *extent.*

The *intensity* of a pleasure or pain is simply how strong the sensation is. It is common these days to see on your doctor's wall a "pain chart" with a scale of 0–10, ranging from no pain sensation to the most intense pain. The doctor asks where on the scale you would put your pain; in identifying a place on the scale, you give your pain a numerical value. *Duration* is the measurement of how long the sensation persists. Pleasure may be highly intense, but fleeting or it may be relatively mild, but long-lasting. As a side note: Bentham seems to have in mind measuring pleasure or pain sensations in terms of standard units of time measurement—minutes, hours, etc. He doesn't factor in the subjective attitudes we have in relation to pleasure and pain that make time feel different. Einstein's famous description of relativity works to illustrate what this means: "Put your hand on a hot stove for a minute, and it seems like an hour. Sit with a pretty girl for an hour, and it seems like a minute." It would be much more difficult, if not impossible, to measure pleasure/pain sensations if that psychological dimension were considered. By *certainty* is meant the likelihood that a pleasure will or will not occur. For instance, we learn through experience what sorts of actions yield which sensations. On that basis we could assign a value to the probability that a pleasurable sensation will occur. *Propinquity* (nearness) is also determined by units of time measurement, how near or how remote is the sensation from the action that produces it. Bentham suggests that these four criteria apply to a pain or pleasure sensation proper. *Fecundity* and *purity* are technically not properties of pleasure or pain but rather are ways to determine the tendency of actions to produce those sensations. *Fecundity* is the term used to describe the probability that a sensation will be followed by sensations of the same sort; *purity* is the probability that a sensation will not be followed by its opposite. *Extent* has to do with the distribution of pleasure or pain among those affected by an action.

Bentham uses his hedonistic calculus not simply for the purpose of quantifying pleasure, but also as what he took to be a purely objective approach to determining morally right actions. The chapter on utilitarianism examines how these criteria could be applied in such a way that we can compare possible courses of actions and outcomes in terms of placing on them a numerical value. Whether that works as a decision procedure for choosing moral actions is the basis for serious criticisms of the Benthamite form of hedonistic utilitarianism.

Though inspired by Bentham's sense that right action is determined by its consequences and that the purpose of morality is to bring about the greatest good for the greatest number, John Stuart Mill had a different understanding of hedonism. Like his predecessor, Mill embraced psychological hedonism, that conception of human nature that says we are constituted so as to desire pleasure and avoid pain, and he adopted the fundamental principles of hedonism; namely, that pleasure is intrinsically good and only pleasure is intrinsically good. But Mill rejected the idea that all pleasures are equal and that they differ only in degrees of magnitude; that is, Mill rejected the quantitative form of hedonism.

Instead, he argued that pleasures differ in terms of quality. Mill writes:

It is quite compatible with the principle of utility to recognize the fact that some kinds of pleasure are more desirable and more valuable than others. It would be absurd that, while, in estimating all other things, quality is considered as well as quantity, the estimation of pleasures should be supposed to depend on quantity alone.[3]

So when we evaluate pleasure, we should consider the kind of pleasure that it is. Here Mill is responding to a common objection to Bentham's approach that hedonism amounts to nothing more than just crass pleasure-seeking.

Mill makes a distinction between *higher* and *lower* pleasures. The lower pleasures are shared by persons and animals, but a person's satisfaction in life requires more than just having pleasurable bodily sensations, however intense or long-lasting these might be. The experience of a higher quality of pleasure employs the use of the higher faculties. The quality of pleasure that satisfies a human is different from that which satisfies an animal. People are capable of more than animals, so it takes more to make a person happy. It doesn't take much, for instance, to satisfy a pig—some mud to roll in, some slop to eat, and the company of other pigs might be all it takes. The enjoyment quotient of a pig is considerably lower than that of a person, particularly in light of the fact that a person may be satisfied in terms of the lower pleasures and yet still feel unfilled. No reasonable person, if given the choice, would consent to leading the life of an animal, even if his or her desire for higher pleasures were unsatisfied. Still some people pursue bodily pleasures at the expense of higher intellectual or emotional ones. The pleasure one experiences from eating chocolate is, no doubt, good but is, in the Millean sense, lower than the intellectual pleasure one might experience, say, from solving a complex problem in mathematics. The pleasure of orgasm is intense, but the experience of it may be richly enhanced by a strong emotional affection felt between sexual partners. About this, Mill famously said: "It is better to be a human being dissatisfied than a pig satisfied; better to be Socrates dissatisfied than a fool satisfied. And if the fool or the pig are of a different opinion, it is because they only know their side of the question."

This last point is crucial. If we experience both kinds of pleasures—the lower and the higher ones—we will continue to pursue the higher ones, not at the expense of satisfying our animal desires, as these are not at odds with our higher capacities, but because they are more commensurate with our faculties and abilities. Moreover, Mill's qualitative approach demonstrates that hedonism is more than a theory about gratifying our brute animal urges. It avoids some of the pitfalls of quantitative hedonism and understands the idea of pleasure in the context of the salient human desire to lead a flourishing life and it views persons as particularly good judges of what it might take to achieve that end.

Nonetheless, Mill's emphasis on the idea that pleasure is the only intrinsic good is problematic. If there is a distinction between higher and lower pleasures and the higher ones are better for us, then it seems that there must be a criterion for making that judgment. And if there is a standard whereby we can distinguish some pleasures as "better" than others, then it follows that there must be something other than pleasure that counts as good. More precisely, if it is better to be Socrates dissatisfied than a fool satisfied, then the experience of pleasure is not all that matters. We often judge some experiences, even those that are less pleasurable than others, as being better for us. In order to make such a judgment at all requires employing a criterion of evaluation other than the feeling of pleasure itself. This apparent inconsistency in qualitative hedonism calls into question at least one of the fundamental theses of hedonism; namely, that pleasure is the only thing that is intrinsically good. It may be that, despite his insistence on the hedonistic conception of the good, Mill supplies the ground for further criticism of hedonism. We turn now to some criticisms of hedonism and a consideration of several alternate conceptions of the good.

Hedonism holds a *monistic* view of the good. This means that there is only one thing that is good in itself. There is, however, no inconsistency in holding that there are things other than pleasure that could qualify as intrinsically good. One could be *pluralistic* with respect to value and suggest that there are many such things—for example, talent, knowledge, beauty, liberty, friendship, happiness. A value *pluralist* may or may not include pleasure in the mix. Either way such a view is not hedonism as it violates one or both of the fundamental theses of hedonism. If one holds that there are many intrinsic goods and pleasure is among them, then she is not a hedonist in that she denies that pleasure is the only intrinsic good. If another holds that there are many intrinsic goods and pleasure is not among them, then he is not a hedonist in that he denies that pleasure is intrinsically good at all. Think again of Finnis's set of basic human goods (discussed in the chapter on moral objectivism)—life, knowledge, play, aesthetic experience, friendship, practical reasonableness, and religion. Each of these is a fundamental good, an intrinsic value, necessary for the good life. Achieving such ends may be accompanied by a feeling of pleasure or satisfaction, but according to Finnis, for instance, their goodness does not rely on that satisfaction; just having them is sufficient. For example, what we want and should pursue is not the satisfaction that might accompany knowledge, though that wouldn't be bad; what we want primarily is knowledge itself.

Now one need not, of course, be a hedonist to reject this idea of the good. That is to say, it may be the case that desire satisfaction must figure in any theory of what counts as good for us, but desire satisfaction is not necessarily construed in terms of pleasure. Suppose, for instance, a person desires to live the life of an ascetic, a self-disciplined life free of pleasurable indulgences. For whatever reasons, this person desires a life of spiritual contemplation and quietude without the distractions of pleasure. It is not the feeling of pleasure that is desired but the contemplation and quietude themselves. Suppose further that the person attains those ends and feels content in having achieved the desired life. Wouldn't we want to say that such a person's life is better for having realized his or her desired ends? The hedonist would think that such a life fails to be better because it lacks the requisite pleasure experiences. A *desire satisfaction theorist*, in contrast to the hedonist, says that the good life is achieved by attaining what we want, even if what we want is not the experience or feeling of pleasure.

There is an obvious problem, however, with saying that the good life is simply getting what you want. Isn't it the case that people are not always good judges and have desires for things that are counterproductive for a good life? Think of the compulsive gambler who desires the thrill of the bet, but who loses his life savings in the process, or the masochist whose desire to be miserable is fulfilled, or the character of Ebenezer Scrooge whose miserly sensibility and desire for money nearly destroys his capacity for even the most ordinary forms of human relationship. In such cases, we judge those lives as precisely the sorts which fail to be made better in virtue of the satisfaction of desire alone. If it is possible to have your desires satisfied and still not have attained a better life, then the desire satisfaction theory fails to provide an adequate conception of what constitutes the good life.

Though non-hedonistic in nature, this argument is structurally similar to Mill's argument against the quantitative form of hedonism. As Mill distinguished between higher and lower pleasures, so here we might distinguish between kinds of desires—those that are more or less conducive to leading a flourishing human life. But in saying this much, it seems necessary that there be a standard for evaluating desires that is something other than the satisfaction of desires itself. We ought to be able to determine which ends are most desirable in the sense that they are most fitting for us as persons.

In this respect, we might think not so much of the mere satisfaction of desires but rather about what it is that gives us fulfilment in life. Two things, both of which have to do with how our desires map on to the world, seem especially important when we consider the conditions of that fulfilment. First, it's not just pleasant experiences or the feeling of being satisfied that matters for fulfilment, it's that the circumstances in the world are such that we can actually do those things that yield the feeling of being satisfied. Second, fulfilment seemingly requires not just the satisfaction of desires but that the satisfaction succeeds in that it accurately reflects the way the world is. Here are two examples from James Rachels[4] to illustrate these points:

1. *A promising young pianist's hands are injured in an automobile accident so that she can no longer play.* Why is this bad for her? Hedonism would say it is bad because it causes her unpleasant feelings. She will feel frustrated and upset whenever she thinks of what might have been and *that* is her misfortune. But doesn't this type of reasoning explain things the wrong way around? It is not as though, by feeling unhappy, she has made an otherwise neutral situation into a bad one. On the contrary, her unhappiness is a rational response to a situation that *is* unfortunate. She could have had a career as a concert pianist, and now she cannot. That is the tragedy. We could not eliminate the tragedy just by getting her to cheer up, that is, by getting her to have pleasant feelings.

2. *You think someone is your friend, but he ridicules you behind your back.* No one tells you, so you never know. Is this unfortunate for you? Hedonism would have to say no because you are never caused any unhappiness. Is something bad still going on?

The first example illustrates the fact that we are not simply content in having good feelings, precisely because it is not simply the feelings that we value. In this case, the pianist values the talent and her unhappiness results from the fact that the circumstances in the world are such that she can longer perform actions that exemplify that talent. The second case illustrates the fact that although good feelings are present, it would still be possible for one's life to be going badly, even if one were unaware of the actual circumstances that obtain in the world. True enough that desires aren't claims about the world, but shouldn't it matter whether the feelings we have in some way reflect the way the world is? Wouldn't the satisfaction you feel in believing that one is your friend when in fact that person undermines the friendship behind your back be illusory in some sense? If so, then it seems that one's fulfilment in life depends not solely on how one feels but, more fundamentally, on how one's feelings succeed in mapping on to the world.

A particularly powerful argument against hedonism comes from the philosopher Robert Nozick. The argument is put forward in the form of a thought-experiment designed to show that we value something other than pleasure and that more things matter to us than just our own internal conscious states. Nozick asks that we imagine an experience machine that would, if we hooked up to it, enable to us to feel anything we desired. Here's how the thought-experiment goes:

> *Suppose there were an experience machine that would give you any experience you desired. Superduper neuropsychologists could stimulate your brain so that you would think and feel you were writing a great novel, or making a friend, or reading an interesting book. All the time you would be floating in a tank with electrodes attached to your brain. Should you plug into this machine for life, preprogramming your life's experiences? If you are worried about missing out on desirable experiences, we can suppose that business enterprises have researched thoroughly the lives of many others. You can pick and choose from their large library or smorgasbord of such experiences, selecting your life's experiences for, say, the next two years. After two years have passed, you will have ten minutes or ten hours out of the tank, to select the experiences of your next two years. Of course, while in the tank you won't know that you're there; you'll think it's all actually happening. Others can also plug in to have the experiences they want, so there's no need to stay unplugged to serve them. (Ignore problems such as who will service the machines if everyone plugs in.) Would you plug in?"[5]*

From a straightforward hedonistic perspective, we should just want to plug into such a machine. After all it's the feeling that counts. Upon further consideration, however, we might come to realize that there are other things that are important to us and wish not to plug into the machine because doing so would prevent us from achieving what really matters. Nozick identifies three such things: 1) we actually want to do certain things; 2) we want to be certain kinds of persons; and 3) we don't want to be limited to an artificial, man-made reality. Take each of these in turn.

1. We actually want to do certain things. Consider again the example of the piano player who loses the use of her hands in a tragic accident. Even if she imagined that she could play the piano, the fact remains that she no longer can. So what is it that she really wants—to feel like she's playing the piano or to be able to play the piano? No amount of time spent hooked up to the experience machine changes the fact that she can no longer perform those actions associated with her talents and her life is made worse off for that reason. The difference between feeling from the inside that one is doing something and actually doing it must make a difference in terms of what makes one's life go better.

2. We want to be certain kinds of persons. If a person were hooked up to the experience machine, he or she would exhibit no signs of personhood, but would be merely a protoplasmic blob. Again the mere experience of being a certain kind of person is distinct from actually being a certain kind of person. Suppose you believe that your life is made better by being a generous person. If your life is to be made better by your being generous, then it isn't sufficient that you just feel as if you have that character trait; one's generosity is manifest in generous acts. Being a certain kind of person actually requires doing certain things—giving to charity, taking care of your children, showing gratitude, etc. While attached to the machine, one is quite literally doing nothing and thus really being no kind of person. Nozick suggests that attachment to the machine is a kind of self-annihilation.

3. We don't want to be limited to an artificial reality; we want real attachments to the world and to other people. The world of the experience machine is substantively no different

than a hallucinatory world. As we maneuver through the actual world and encounter real people, we modify our judgments, re-organize our desires, and adjust our projects and plans accordingly. This kind of reflective process is conducive to our fulfillment and requires that we experience the world as it is.

Now are these things important to us because we want them, as a desire satisfaction theorist would suggest; or do we want them for some reason regarding their nature? That is, do our lives go better because in having such things we feel satisfied? Or do our lives go better because those things are worth having? Nozick takes the latter position. In a comment on his own thought-experiment written several years after its first appearance, Nozick writes:

> *Notice that I am not saying simply that since we desire connection to actuality the experience machine is defective because it does not give us what we desire ... for that would make "getting whatever you desire" the primary standard. Rather, I am saying that the connection to actuality is important whether or not we desire it—that is why we desire it— and the experience machine is inadequate because it doesn't give us that.[6]*

The argument here is that the connection to the actual world is an objective good in itself and so for that reason is desirable and ought to be desired. The experience machine disallows the connection and that is why hooking up to it thwarts the possibility of human fulfillment.

Under this view, the condition for the possibility of achieving the good life is that we confront the world as it actually is. We could have pleasurable experiences and satisfied desires that bear no attachment to the circumstances that obtain in the world. If we took those to be what has ultimate value for us, we would seemingly have to deny that actually doing things, being certain kinds of persons, and living in a natural world with others have any bearing on our well-being and happiness. Human fulfillment would be nothing more than the sum total of pleasurable experiences or satisfied desires. If, however, we believe that our fulfillment depends on our complex connection to the actual world and our attachments to others, then we are more likely to view happiness as a characteristically human achievement.

ENDNOTES

1. Peter Singer, ed. *Ethics* (Oxford University Press, 1994). See Singer's introduction to the section on Ultimate Good, p. 179.

2. Jeremy Bentham, *The Rationale of Reward* (originally published in 1825) in Singer, *Ethics*, p. 200.

3. John Stuart Mill, *Utilitarianism* (originally published in 1861); see Chapter 2 "What Utilitarianism Is." Reference here is from *The Philosophy of John Stuart Mill* edited by Marshall Cohen (Modern Library, 1961), pp. 331–332.

4. Stuart Rachels, *The Elements of Moral Philosophy* Eighth Edition (McGraw Hill, 2015), pp. 112–113.

5. Robert Nozick, *Anarchy, State, and Utopia* (Basic Books, 1974), pp. 43–45.

6. Robert Nozick, *The Examined Life: Philosophical Meditations* (Touchstone Books, 1990), pp. 106–107.

STUDY QUESTIONS

7. Distinguish between *instrumental* and *intrinsic goods*.

8. What role does consciousness play with respect to the concept of the good?

9. What is *hedonism*?

10. Explain Jeremy Bentham's *quantitative hedonism*. What is the *hedonistic calculus?*

11. Describe John Stuart Mill's *qualitative hedonism*. In what significant ways does Mill's theory differ from Bentham's? How does Mill distinguish between *higher* and *lower* pleasures?

12. Hedonism is a *monistic* view of the good. What does that mean? What is *value pluralism*?

13. What is *desire satisfaction theory*? How does it differ from hedonism?

14. How do Rachels and Nozick argue against hedonistic and desire-satisfaction theories?

QUESTIONS FOR REFLECTION

1. Do you think there is an ultimate good for us? If so, what is it?

2. Consider the question, "*Is it better to be a satisfied pig or a dissatisfied Socrates?*" How would Bentham and Mill answer the question? Who do you think has the better answer and why?

3. Is the good just a matter of feeling pleasure? Is it a matter of satisfying desires? Something else? Could your life be going badly even if you feel good or are satisfied? Is feeling good always what we want? (Think of Rachels's examples.)

4. Review Nozick's thought experiment about the *experience machine.* Would you connect to the machine? Why or why not?

SUGGESTIONS FOR FURTHER READING

Bramble, Ben. "The Experience Machine." *Philosophy Compass* 11 (3), 2016.

Crisp, Roger. "Pleasure Is All That Matters." *Think* 3 (7), 2004.

Feldman, Fred. *What is This Thing Called Happiness?*. Oxford: Oxford University Press, 2010.

Feldman, Fred. *Pleasure and the Good Life: Concerning the Nature, Varieties and Plausibility of Hedonism.* Oxford: Clarendon Press, 2004.

Fletcher, Guy, ed. *The Routledge Handbook of Philosophy of Well-Being.* Routledge, 2016.

Moore, G. E. *Principia Ethica.* Cambridge: Cambridge University Press, 1903.

Parfit, Derek. *Reasons and Persons.* Oxford: Oxford University Press, 1984.

Ross, W. D. *The Right and the Good.* Oxford: Clarendon Press, 1930.

CHAPTER 6
Duty

When you think about morality, do you think more about desires, inclinations, making people feel good, and bringing about good consequences, or do you think more about duty, rules, intentions, and the quality of certain actions themselves? Do you think that actions serve as means to some end or do you think of actions as being simply right or wrong? If someone poses a question like, "Is it wrong to lie?" are you more likely to answer, "That depends," or "Absolutely, it's always wrong to lie"? Do you think our moral reason is limited by our natural desires and our ability to predict consequences of our actions or do you believe that moral reason is independent of human desire and can lead us to understand why certain actions are right or wrong in themselves? Do you think actions are only right or wrong in terms of what they achieve or fail to achieve, or do you think that what one intends to do matters in our moral assessment of actions? Do you think we could be "negatively responsible" for the consequences of someone else's action or do you think we are uniquely responsible for our own actions?

The collection of these questions is designed to show the stark contrast between consequentialist theories like utilitarianism and deontological moral theories or duty ethics. Deontology (from the Greek *deon,* meaning obligation or duty) is the philosophical term used to refer to the kind of moral theory in which the concept of duty is fundamental. Under this view, the rightness or wrongness of actions is not dependent on outcomes, but rather is intrinsic to an action itself. We have duties to perform right actions and duties to refrain from performing wrong actions. Since deontology rejects the idea that consequences justify the claim that an action is morally right or morally wrong, it requires a different form of justification, one that provides us with a way of knowing just what kinds of actions are duties. In this regard, the concept of moral rightness takes priority over the concept of good. It is the task of deontology to explain why this is so and how it is that we have moral obligations or duties at all. For the deontologist, moral obligations are objective in the sense that they apply to all persons, and so it is important also to account for the general applicability of moral principles.

Consider too that there is a deontological aspect to our everyday moral experience. Many people believe that it is necessary to meet the demands of their moral principles and do the right thing, even if it doesn't generate pleasure or happiness for themselves or others. Our desires to experience good things sometimes run counter to what we know is right to do on some occasion. This is not to suggest that the desire for pleasure or happiness is bad, or that those things are bad in themselves, but rather that what is morally right is independent of those things and our desire for them. It is also not to suggest that desire and duty are necessarily at odds or that doing what is right somehow requires feelings of displeasure. In an ideal moral universe, desires and duties would always coincide. The point again is that we don't derive our duties from our desires, and outcomes do not provide a reason for claiming that an action is right.

This is another way of viewing the contrast between deontology and consequentialism. Think of Bentham and Mill and their idea that morality is rooted in the fact that we desire pleasure and pleasure alone is what is desirable. Under their view, moral reason is limited to figuring out the best way to achieve the goal of bringing about the greatest good for the greatest number. Deontology holds an opposing view; the problem of morality is to determine what is right, and if we could accomplish that, then an even more challenging problem emerges: Assuming we know the right thing to do, why should we do it? The answer might simply be "because it's right." Moreover, we can know this in advance with some measure of certainty; there is no need to wait until the results are in, so to speak, before we have a clear sense of moral rightness.

If it's not the desire to bring about good consequences that constitutes moral motivation, then what should the moral motive be to do the right thing? Here deontologists often appeal to the concept of intention. In performing a morally right action one might intend certain consequences, but if consequences are not the determinant of rightness, then in having that intention one is not necessarily performing an action because it is the right thing. What if the consequences were different? What if a morally wrong action was more likely to bring about the desired ends? Here's an example to illustrate the point: Suppose Cynthia gives to charity, and does so in order to benefit from a tax deduction. Her motive here is self-interested and her intention in performing the act is to reap some benefit. She is not motivated to act because of the goodness of charitable giving, but because of what she stands to gain. Now suppose the tax deduction is taken away. So goes Cynthia's motive, but the goodness of charitable giving still remains. Cynthia realizes she can reap the same financial benefit by cheating on her taxes. Since she is motivated by self-interest and intends to perform the action because it benefits her, then she is likely to cheat on her taxes. But just as the lack of benefit doesn't change the intrinsic goodness of the act of charitable giving, so neither does the benefit Cynthia receives from cheating on her taxes change the intrinsic wrongness of that act. An action is right even without good consequences and an action is wrong even with good consequences.

We should then be motivated to act because an action is a duty; moral rightness itself should be the object of our intention. Actions are right or wrong in terms of whether they adhere to a clear moral rule; but for an action to have moral value it must be performed by a person whose intention is to do that action because it is the right thing to do. We certainly hold people responsible when they intend to perform morally wrong actions. That's just a clear case of immorality in both the action and in the bad intentions of the person. Deontology, as presented thus far, goes further in suggesting that right actions done for the wrong reasons (with improper motives and misdirected intentions) effectively lose their moral value. Adherence to a moral rule is a necessary but not a sufficient condition for one's actions to have moral value. It's important to see, then, that actions aren't made right by intentions. We couldn't just use intentions, for instance, to absolve a person of responsibility for performing evil deeds precisely because a person's full moral responsibility requires the recognition that an action is a duty. This, as we will see, is an essential aspect of the Kantian version of duty ethics.

In his highly influential work, *The Foundations of the Metaphysics of Morals* written in 1785, Immanuel Kant (1724–1804) argues that the foundation of morality is rationality itself.

There he systematically attempts to demonstrate that moral duty cannot be derived from our natural tendencies, psychological inclinations, or subjective desires; nor could it be gotten on the basis of some idea of what outcomes our actions might produce. Instead duty must be grounded in reason itself. For Kant, morality requires that we act freely, that we choose to perform actions that we recognize to be morally good. We would be incapable of rationally choosing to act if there were conditions that imposed constraints on us from the outside. For Kant, morality requires that we be autonomous, self-directed agents.

In this chapter we will focus on Kant's approach as a paradigmatic example of deontological moral theory. Before considering Kant's view specifically, it is worth mentioning that there are other kinds of deontological theories, each of which attempts to explain how moral duties are to be understood. Here are several versions:

1. *The Divine Command Theory*: The divine command theory says that an action is morally right or wrong because it is commanded by God and because God commands it we are under a moral obligation to do or refrain from doing what the command requires. So we ought to perform actions simply because they are duties as determined by God; whether or not they are consistent with our desires or bring about good consequences.

2. *Natural Law Ethics*: Natural law theory argues that there are certain things that are good for us by nature, and reason, the defining characteristic of human nature, tells us what they are. Moral or practical reasoning leads us to an understanding of what actions are required to achieve and sustain those goods; we have a duty to perform such actions. This is not to be confused with utilitarianism, where the concern is to bring about the best overall consequences for the greatest number. In contrast, the natural law theorist believes that fundamental goods are inherent in nature and so the actions that sustain those goods are absolutely required. Thomas Aquinas (1225–1274), for instance, argues that on the basis of this use of reason we can derive a general and fundamental principle of morality: "Do good and avoid evil." In applying this general principle to specific goods we can come up with moral rules that apply universally—this is the deontological element in natural law ethical theory. For example, life is a natural good. Morality would require us, then, to perform actions that are life-sustaining and avoid those that prevent the realization of or destroy that good. So on the basis of the general principle cited above, we could deduce that an action like murder is wrong, and not just sometimes, but universally. Note that natural law ethics is a mixed view. It does define the right in terms of a prior understanding of the good, but unlike consequentialism, it believes we can determine moral obligations in advance.

3. *Natural Rights Theory*: Natural rights theory suggests that, by nature, human beings are endowed with certain rights that are inalienable and that form the basis of our moral relationships to each other. John Locke (1632–1704), for instance, identified such rights as life, liberty, and property. The deontological component here is that the rights of individuals impose obligations on others. If one has a right to life, then this minimally requires that we refrain from any actions which violate that right; one has a right not to be killed and this imposes an obligation on us not to kill; if one has a right to property, then we have an obligation not to steal, and so on. Moral duty is thus determined by the constraints that rights impose on our actions.

Kant rejects all of these kinds of theory, not because he disbelieves in God, or that he thinks there are no natural goods, or that he believes we have no rights. His point is that the ground for moral obligation is to be found in rationality alone, free from the constraints that nature imposes on us as human beings and independent even of God's commands, which in order to bind us morally would be rational themselves. Let's turn now to a discussion of the central ideas in Kant's moral theory.

KANTIAN MORAL THEORY

Kant's project is guided by the fundamental idea that if morality matters at all, it can only be because we are rational and free. Though there is much in human life that is subject to our desires, morality must, in some sense, be independent of those desires. The idea of freedom that serves as the basis for morality is not one that can be understood in terms of what we "want" to do, but rather needs to be understood in terms of what we "ought" to do. That is, Kant advocates the idea that freedom involves choosing to do what one rationally knows to be one's duty.

On the face of it, this is difficult to grasp because duty imposes a kind of necessity on us—an obligation to do or refrain from doing certain things. It would seem that this necessity conflicts with freedom in that obligation restricts our actions. Kant has it the other way around. True moral freedom is unrestricted by anything in nature, by our desires, by expected outcomes of actions, etc. Freedom is manifest in our rational capacity to choose morality (duty) for ourselves. Our rational nature is in essence our autonomy—the idea that we can impose the moral law on ourselves. Note further that this means we can choose not to obey the dictates of moral reason, but we can't so choose and at the same time expect that our actions would have any moral value. This imposes on each of us a singularly unique moral responsibility to choose the right thing for the right reason. Moreover, this sense of moral freedom serves as a foundation for the universality of moral principles and duties. Rationality, though manifest in one's own choices, belongs to no one in particular. The rules it uncovers are rules that apply to everyone, irrespective of specific circumstances and situations. For Kant all of this adds up to the fundamental reason why we ought to choose to obey moral duty; namely, that in doing so we respect persons—ourselves and others—as rational, autonomous agents. In fine, Kant argues that morality is only possible for beings that are rational in this sense.

What follows is a brief summary of how Kant attempts to establish this idea of morality, with a focus on three important Kantian concepts: The good will, the categorical imperative, and respect for persons.

THE GOOD WILL

Kant begins with the idea that a good will is the only thing that can be thought of as good without qualification or good in itself.[1] This does not mean that there are no other things that are good for us; there are plenty of such things. Kant, himself, identifies such goods as *talents of the mind* like intelligence, wit, and prudence, or *qualities of temperament* like courage, resoluteness, and perseverance, and *blessings of fortune* like power, wealth, honor, health, and happiness. These are undoubtedly good things or traits to have, but the mere possession of them does not make the possessor good. This is to say that none of these things nor all of them combined measure up to something that is good without qualification. You can think, for instance, of an intelligent, witty, resolute, healthy **bank robber.** Or you can imagine an intelligent, prudent, perseverant, resolute, powerful, wealthy, healthy **tyrant.** It is evident that one can have these goods and use them for incredible evil. They are only good if qualified by a good will, a will that is directed solely toward moral goodness.

Certain emotional states seem especially well-designed for a good will—e.g., self-control and calm deliberation—and we generally admire such traits. Even these, however, are not unconditionally good and are admirable only if they are informed by a good will. If not informed by a good will, they "may become extremely bad." For instance, Kant says that "the coolness of a villain makes him not only far more dangerous but also more directly abominable in our eyes than he would have seemed without it."[2]

How, then, should we understand the idea that the good will is good without qualification? Here's Kant's sense of it. The good will is that will which chooses to act for the sole reason that it recognizes an action as the right thing to do. Much of Kant's moral philosophy is an expansion of the ideas contained in that statement. The good will *chooses.* In this sense, the good will is not defined by an emotional feeling, but by the exercise of freedom. So the good will is a free will. But it's not that the good will chooses whatever it wants. Our psychology tendencies, nature inclinations, and desires are better suited to get us what we want. To say that the good will is free is to say that it chooses to perform right actions. The good will is also a rational will. On the basis of reason, the good will *recognizes* that an action is the right thing to do. Finally, the good will is a will that has a proper motive or intention. It chooses to act *because* (for the reason that) an action is the right thing to do. Why do the right thing? Because it's the right thing. The good will, Kant says, has duty as its motive. The good will is a free, rational, and properly motivated will.

From this perspective, the good will is good in itself because it is impossible for it to choose anything other than what is morally right. It lays down the necessary and sufficient conditions for our actions to have moral value. This is to say that if a person has a good will, that person's actions would have moral worth in virtue of that will alone; and without a good will, a person's actions could not have moral worth. So the moral worth of actions is not determined by consequences.

In Kant's view, consequences neither add to nor subtract from the inherent value of the good will, since the good will is defined completely independent of any good or bad results that may be produced by our actions. Good consequences, for oneself or for the general welfare, could be produced by means other than moral action. A good will would thus be unnecessary if morality were founded on the satisfaction of desires or for the improvement of conditions in the world. Not even happiness counts as the ultimate goal of action; it is not the point of morality. Instead Kant suggests if one performs right actions for the right reason, then one is worthy of happiness even if one is not actually happy. By the same token, it is impossible to know the moral law without the rationality of a good will, since the very purpose of moral reason is to come to know what our moral obligations are. Morality is the exclusive province of rational beings. Any rational being—a human person or any other kind of being with the capacity to develop an autonomous good will—is bound by and judged by the same moral rules.

In choosing to perform an action because it is a duty, the good will makes duty its motive. In this sense, it is not sufficient simply to perform an action that happens to be in accordance with duty. Rather, to make duty the motive is, as Kant puts it, "to act from duty." So an action may be in accordance with duty, but still not be done with duty as the motive.

Here's an example to illustrate the distinction: Tom, Dick, and Harry are students in a moral philosophy class and they have written papers on Kant's moral theory. Tom and Harry submitted original work and both received reasonably good grades. Dick plagiarized his paper, was caught and received a failing grade for the course. Tom and Harry discuss Dick's action and agree that he got what he deserved, as he clearly did something wrong. Tom says that he wouldn't plagiarize because he fears getting caught and wouldn't want to suffer the same fate as Dick. Harry wonders whether Tom has learned anything from studying Kant and proclaims that's no reason not to plagiarize. He says the only reason not to plagiarize is to recognize that plagiarism is a form of dishonesty and one has a moral obligation to be honest. In other words, Harry says he didn't plagiarize because it's wrong to do so. It should be evident that Dick was just plain dishonest, and it seems clear enough that Harry and Tom both did the right thing. But did both of them act honestly?

Here's a trim Kantian analysis: Tom acted on the basis of an inclination not to get caught and a desire to avoid punishment. But what if he were sure he wouldn't get caught and could thus be certain that he would be spared the discomfort of any punishment? It might be, with those conditions no longer operative, that Tom would have plagiarized. Harry acted without regard to the consequences; his action was motivated by the rational judgment that plagiarism is downright dishonest. Harry's action meets the criteria of Kant's good will, but Tom's action does not. The Kantian conclusion is that Harry's action has moral worth, but Tom's does not. Notice further the full and rather stringent judgment that this involves. Harry is an honest person, but Tom is not. Tom, though his action was right, gets no more moral credit than Dick, whose action was clearly wrong.

Many might feel troubled by all this, particularly the last conclusion. After all, isn't it the case that doing the right thing, even if for the wrong reason, is preferable to doing the wrong thing? Kant's answer is a clear and resounding NO. The only way one would be inclined to say so is if consequences mattered in the determination of moral rightness, and recall if that were the case then rationality would not be required for moral action. In fine, Harry acted freely and rationally, but Tom did not.

It should be evident, then, that the reason one has for acting is crucial in the determination of moral value. The specific reason or rule or simple argument one gives for acting is what Kant calls a *maxim*. Kant is not saying that if we act on inclination, then the action we perform cannot be right. What he is saying is that inclination could never suffice as a moral reason for acting. The reason is that if you try to frame your maxim in terms of your inclinations, then you would have a rule that applies only to you. Since morality lays down universal obligations, then the maxim of your action ought to be one that any person could adopt. It is possible, for instance, to universalize the idea that one should always act honestly. Could the same be said for something like the following: Act honestly only when not doing so brings about bad consequences for you? If that were the rule, then one would have no reason to act honestly, if there were no bad consequences in acting dishonestly. But how would we know when our maxims determined our moral duties? In order to answer this, we turn to a discussion of Kant's supreme moral principle—the categorical imperative.

THE CATEGORICAL IMPERATIVE[3]

Rules for acting are framed as imperatives or commands that tell us what to do and they are common in our everyday experience. "Take the 7:45 train!" "Brush your teeth!" "Shut the window!" "Study calculus!" "Zip up your fly!" There is an important aspect to these imperatives; namely, they are conditioned on some goal or other one wishes to achieve. For instance:

"Take the 7:45 train to ensure that you get to Grand Central Station by 9:00."
"Brush your teeth so you don't get cavities."
"Shut the window so it doesn't get too cold in the room."
"Study calculus so you can get your engineering degree."
"Zip up your fly so your date doesn't think you're a slob or a pervert."

These imperatives apply to particular persons in specific situations. They pertain only in those circumstances where a particular person has a desire or inclination to reach some specified goal. They really go shorthand for conditional statements like: "If you want an engineering degree, then study calculus," or "If you want to be at Grand Central Station by 9:00, then take the 7:45 train," and so on. Kant calls these *hypothetical imperatives*. A hypothetical imperative is conditional in the sense that it depends on certain things, and tells us what needs to be done in order to attain some desired objective. A hypothetical imperative, like any command, is a rule of reason, but it dictates an action which is good only as a means to something else; it does not command us to perform an action which is good in itself. Indeed, it would certainly be odd to say something like "it is always right to take the 7:45 train." What if you don't need to be at Grand Central Station until 2:00 or what if you don't need or wish to be there at all?

Kant argues that hypothetical imperatives cannot function as moral imperatives. This is not to deny their value, as it is clear that we live by these sorts of imperatives on a daily basis. Rather, in setting up conditions, hypothetical imperatives do not command absolutely. For Kant, moral actions are not means to ends, but are just right or wrong in themselves. So he says that moral imperatives must command absolutely, with no conditions attached. He calls this kind of command the *categorical imperative*. In Kant's duty-based moral theory, the categorical imperative is what he considers to be the "supreme principle of morality." The categorical imperative is *unconditional* in that it commands absolutely without any reference to any consequence of an action. It applies to moral actions and determines the necessity of performing an action; that is, it determines an action to be a moral duty. It derives from rationality itself and is an expression of our autonomy as moral agents. Reason tells us what the moral law is and we impose that law on ourselves; this is the function of the good will in Kant's sense.

As Kant understands it, the categorical imperative is a general command and is used as a kind of test procedure for determining what specific actions qualify as moral duties. It says whatever action you take, if it is to qualify as a moral action, must exemplify certain inherent qualities. Specifically it must be the kind of action that does not depend on your particular interests or desires or goals, that is consistently performable in any circumstance whatsoever, that any rational person would perform, and that respects persons as rational, autonomous agents. This is best understood in terms of how the categorical imperative is formulated. Kant gives several formulations, two of which are as follows:

1. The Principle of Universalizability: *Act as if the maxim of your action were to become through your will a universal law of nature.*
2. The Principle of Respect for Persons: *Act in such a way that you always treat humanity, whether in your own person or in the person of any other, never simply as a means, but always at the same time as an end.*

Though these are different versions of the categorical imperative, they are not different commands just different expressions of the same command. They fundamentally say the same thing—always do what is right. In these formulations what is right is understood to be that which we can consistently will to be universal and that which respects persons as having value in themselves.

To see how the categorical imperative is used as a test procedure for determining what specific actions qualify as moral duties consider the principle of universalizability. To test for universalizability we can ask: "What would happen if everyone did this?" or, "Would it be okay for anyone to do this in the same or similar circumstances?" If what I am about to do is morally correct then, for Kant, it would be morally correct for everyone to do the same thing. This is precisely what it means for an action to be universalizable; that is, it is good for anyone and everyone, everywhere, at any time. More specifically, the categorical imperative says you should be *willing* to say that a moral rule applies to everyone, yourself included. You cannot be exempt from the demands of morality or expected to be treated differently than any other person. So for instance, if you are not willing to allow others to lie to you, then you ought not lie to others. Moreover, the rule must be applied consistently, if a rule leads to a contradiction, then it cannot be a valid moral rule. Suppose I wish to lie. If I will that lying become a universal law, then I must be prepared to say that it is logically possible that everyone can be lying all the time. But does that make logical sense? If I say that all persons are liars, then either I'm lying or telling the truth. If I'm telling the truth, then it can't be true that all persons are liars. If I'm lying, then it wouldn't be true that all persons are liars. Under such a circumstance no one could ever know who's lying and who's not; it would no longer be possible to trust anything anyone ever says. Kant famously concludes, "I can will to lie, but I cannot will that lying become a universal law." There is no inconsistency in willing that everyone be honest; truth-telling, for instance, can be universalized.

Kant distinguishes between two classes of duties. He calls these *perfect duties* and *imperfect duties*. *Perfect duties* are such that they can be universally willed and in breaking them we could clearly see a logical contradiction and would quite positively be disrespecting persons—ourselves or others. These are sometimes called *negative* duties in that they can be expressed as prohibitions such as don't murder; don't lie; don't steal; don't commit suicide. A rational will understands that we must never do such things because we could not will such acts as murder or lying or stealing or suicide to be universal, and in doing such things we would be treating persons as means to our own ends. *Imperfect duties* are not as specific as perfect duties in that they are broad imperatives that require us to use our wills in determining just how to obey them. These are sometimes called *positive* duties because to obey them requires more than just refraining from performing certain acts, it requires doing certain things.

When we disobey perfect duties, we clearly do something disrespectful to persons. In disobeying imperfect duties, we may not be actively disrespecting ourselves or others as in the case of breaking perfect duties, but neither would we be respecting those persons. Consider that we have an imperfect duty to help others in need or a duty to develop our talents. There are many ways to do these things and so we must decide for ourselves how best to meet those demands. It's easy to figure how not to murder someone, quite another matter to decide how to help someone. There is certainly a difference between setting a homeless man on fire and indifferently passing by him sitting on a park bench every day. If someone sets a homeless person on fire, that is a clear violation of a perfect duty. It's not simply that he has done nothing to help the homeless man, he has done something atrociously harmful. If you indifferently pass by, you are not actively doing anything to harm him, but neither are you doing anything actively to help him; this may constitute a violation of an imperfect duty. Also, we could imagine that no one ever obeyed imperfect duties; that is, disobedience to them does not issue in a straightforward logical contradiction. It's quite possible, for instance, that everyone could be lazy in a way that it is not possible for everyone to be a liar. But would you think of a world in which no one ever developed his or her talents to be a sufficiently robust moral community? With respect to perfect duties, we **couldn't** consistently will that breaking those duties be universalized; with respect to imperfect duties a rational person **wouldn't** will that breaking them be universalized. A rational person wouldn't will a world in which no one developed his talents and no one helped anyone in need, despite the fact that such a world may be logically possible. For Kant, both types of duties are required for the moral life. Morality requires not simply refraining from doing bad things, but actively doing good things as well, and the application of the categorical imperative determines what those duties are.

RESPECT FOR PERSONS

The second formulation of the categorical imperative, the principle of respect for persons, provides perhaps the best way of understanding the fullest expression of Kant's moral theory. In his view, persons have value and dignity in themselves and are thus worthy of respect.[4] This value is intrinsic and does not derive from any empirical circumstances, whether external situations or internal inclinations. What matters from the moral point of view is that persons are rational and free, and as such deserve to be treated as equal members of a moral community. A person's value comes not from being a member of a species, but from having the capacity to rationally determine duties and to be self-legislating autonomous agents. Any being that had such capacities would qualify, in Kant's sense, as a person and would count as a member of a universal moral community, what he refers to as a "kingdom of ends."

It might seem that Kant is denying a simple fact of our existence in saying that we should not treat persons as a means to an end. After all, don't we use the waitress in a restaurant as a means to get our food, or the mechanic as a means to repair our cars, or the musician as a means to please our ears, and so forth? On more careful examination, however, we find that Kant acknowledges this fact. His point is that we should never **simply** or **merely** use persons as means. It is possible to use people in the ways described above and still respect them and allow them to use us. The waitress brings our food, but she gets paid and we give her a tip. We use the mechanic to repair our car, but he uses us as the source of his livelihood. We use the musician for our pleasure, but he takes pleasure in playing to a large audience. We do these things out of mutual cooperation or perhaps even with a kind of mutual respect. What the Kantian view prohibits is using persons as if they were mere things.

When we use persons as things we deny their intrinsic value as rational, autonomous beings. We turn them into tools or devices used for the purpose of benefitting ourselves, where the other is incapacitated from benefitting from any mutual cooperation or participating in a community of mutual respect. Kidnapping a person and holding her for ransom, depriving someone of his liberty and using him as a slave, committing date rape, or stealing another person's property are all clear instances of using other persons as things. No rational person would consent to being a slave, a kidnap or rape victim, or to having his or her property stolen. But think also of more ordinary experiences. Jack and Jill have been dating for a while. Jill loves Jack, but Jack is just not sure about his feelings for Jill. They both need a place to live. Jill says she'd be happy to move in with Jack if he swears that he loves her. Jack's desperate for an affordable apartment and moving into a place with Jill would be ideal. He swears undying love, and Jill believes him. They get the apartment together. By trading on her trust and using it to his own advantage, Jack really views Jill as part of a real estate deal. (Coda: It is later revealed that Jack is a habitual liar and a cheat and Jill learns this and uncovers his self-regarding motive about the apartment; she's devastated.) We might say, of course, that this doesn't rise to the level of rape or kidnapping. Nonetheless, we should acknowledge that lying and capitalizing on a person's trust violate a person's autonomy just the same. It seems likely that a rational person would no more consent to being lied to and used in this fashion than she would consent to being a victim of date rape. This, at least, seems to be the implication of Kant's view and it reminds us that mutual respect is necessary in the everyday aspects of our lives.

Some may argue that Kant's deontological moral theory is too stringent in that it allows for no exceptions to the moral rules we discover. Shouldn't we make exceptions when doing so would make the world a better place? But maybe this is to miss the whole point. How much better a place could the world be than if everyone were obeying the Kantian perfect duties—not murdering, not stealing, keeping promises, etc.—and determining how best to fulfill the imperfect duties, doing all they can to develop their own talents and to help others in need? As ideal as Kant's notion of the "kingdom of ends" may sound, it leaves out certain salient aspects of the moral life. It excludes any reference to the development of human emotions and the role they play in our being able to respond sensitively to the moral demands of particular circumstances; it denies any moral value to actual happiness; and it conceives of duty as completely independent of and in no way constituted by a characteristically human desire to be and to do good.

ENDNOTES

1. Immanuel Kant, *The Foundations of the Metaphysics of Morals*. References here are to *The Foundations of the Metaphysics of Morals* translated by Lewis White Beck with Critical

Essays Edited by Robert Paul Wolff (Bobbs-Merrill, 1982). In the first section of this work, Kant argues that morality is founded on a rational will, the only thing that is good without qualification. The good will is the source of our sense of moral duty.

2. Kant, p. 12.

3. See Kant, *The Foundations of the Metaphysics of Morals*. This section is a summary of ideas contained in section two of that work. There Kant argues that moral rules command unconditionally and derive from a supreme moral principle he calls the "categorical imperative." This principle is derived from rationality itself and not the particular characteristics of human nature—desires, inclinations, tendencies, etc. It would apply to any rational being. Kant distinguishes the categorical imperative from hypothetical imperatives that lay out conditions necessary to reach certain specified goals; the latter are not moral commands. Kant also gives several formulations of the categorical imperative, two of which—the principle of universalizability and the principle of respect for persons—are discussed here.

4. Note that for Kant the term 'person' does not mean the same thing as 'human being.' Any rational, autonomous being qualifies as a person. 'Human being' is a term that refers to our nature as determined by natural, empirical conditions. A human being is a natural thing; a person is not a thing but a value in and of itself.

STUDY QUESTIONS

5. What is *deontology*?

6. Describe the different kinds of deontological theories.

7. Explain Kant's concept of the good will. Consider the concepts of rationality, free will/ autonomy, and duty as the moral motive. Is the good will the only thing that is good? Why does Kant say that good will is the only thing that is good *in itself*?

8. What is the difference between *hypothetical* and *categorical imperatives*?

9. What is a maxim?

10. Describe the *principle of universalizability* and the *principle of respect for persons.*

11. How is the categorical imperative used as a test procedure for determining moral duty?

12. Explain the difference between *perfect* and *imperfect duties.*

13. How does Kant distinguish between persons and things?

QUESTIONS FOR REFLECTION

1. For Kant, lying is always wrong no matter what the circumstances. What do you think? Can you imagine any circumstances when it might be morally permissible to lie? Give an example.

2. According to Kant, actions done out of inclination and without the intention to act on duty have no moral worth, even if they conform to duty. Do you think this is right? Do intentions matter that much?

3. Kant argues that because persons have value in themselves, we have a moral duty to treat persons with respect. Animals aren't persons. Does that mean we should treat animals as mere things, as Kant's theory implies? Do we have any moral obligations toward animals? What might a utilitarian say?

SUGGESTIONS FOR FURTHER READING

Aune, Bruce. *Kant's Theory of Morals*. Princeton: Princeton University Press, 1979.

Darwall, Stephen L., ed. *Deontology*. Oxford: Basil Blackwell, 2002.

Donagan, Alan. *The Theory of Morality*. Chicago: University of Chicago Press, 1977.

Korsgaard, Christine M. *Creating the Kingdom of Ends*. Cambridge: Cambridge University Press, 1996.

Langton, Rae. "Duty and Desolation." *Philosophy* 67, 1992.

O'Neill, Onora. *Acting on Principle*. New York: Columbia University Press, 1975.

Paton, H. J. *The Categorical Imperative*. Pennsylvania: University of Pennsylvania, 1947.

Schneewind, J. B. *Essays on the History of Moral Philosophy*. Oxford: Oxford University Press, 2010.

CHAPTER 7
Virtue

Is the moral life taken up exclusively, or even primarily, with trying to determine which actions are right or wrong? From the perspective of normative ethical theories like utilitarianism and deontology, it would seem to be the case that we meet the demands of morality simply by adopting and applying the criteria for moral correctness. For utilitarianism, we only need to perform actions that bring about the best overall outcomes in order for those actions to qualify as morally good ones. Under that view, morality is solely a matter of improving the circumstances in the world, making it a better place by producing good consequences for the greatest number; intentions just don't matter. Kant's duty ethics provides a supreme moral principle—the categorical imperative—the application of which tests whether the rules we follow in acting can be universalized, whether an action counts as a duty. Under this view, the intention to perform an action because it is a duty is what exclusively determines the moral value of the action; consequences don't matter.

Because utilitarianism is concerned with overall happiness, it places no value on any one individual's happiness. Kantianism, too, places no value on an individual's happiness, not because it is overridden by a sense of the general welfare or because the individual cancels out, but because happiness is not the point of morality at all. There's a dilemma that emerges when we consider these two views in juxtaposition. On the one hand, there is a broad and sweeping notion of happiness without any recognition of the value of one's own personal qualities and ends. On the other hand, there is a large, looming notion of the moral agent, the individual, completely devoid of desires, natural inclinations, tendencies, and traits. When put in these terms, we may wonder whether either perspective could possibly portray morality as we live it in everyday life.

One reason the dilemma emerges at all is that both sides ignore something that seems so naturally a part of the moral life—a person's character. Character is understood not in some abstract sense as a general interest in producing a better world or as rational intention, but rather as a full measure of a person's reasons, desires, emotions, and dispositions—how they are organized in oneself and how they relate to a person's action. This is the focus of virtue ethics. Whereas consequentialist and deontological ethical theories are primarily concerned with identifying universal moral principles and determining how and when actions are morally right or wrong, virtue ethics is concerned more fundamentally with the development of a virtuous character. "What is the good life?" and "What kind of person should one be?" are the central questions of virtue ethics.

Virtue ethics, like consequentialism and deontology, is a normative ethical theory; in this regard it purports to be action-guiding. Unlike those theories, however, virtue ethics does not endeavor to identify a general moral principle like the utilitarian greatest happiness principle or the Kantian principle of universalizability; instead it seeks to understand what good character is and how that character informs our actions. Moral action cannot be understood in isolation from the kind of person one is, so the task of virtue ethics is to identify those traits of character that are exemplified in the virtuous person. So when we are considering what to do in a particular circumstance, we should ask: "What would the virtuous person do in this case?" We can think of this question in more specific terms when we consider particular virtues like courage or generosity. So we might ask "what would the courageous person do?" or "what would the generous person do?" Such questions are more complicated than they may initially appear to be in that they require we know what the virtues are, what it means to possess those virtues, and how it is that they lead to certain actions.

It is evident in ordinary life that not everyone is virtuous in exactly the same way. Virtue ethics, then, has to account for the wide variability of ways in which people can exhibit moral goodness. At the same time, it provides a context for understanding what virtue is, in general, and for understanding the purpose of leading a virtuous life at all. These are central points in Aristotle's conception of virtue as contained in his *Nichomachean Ethics,* the main focus of this chapter.[1]

ARISTOTLE'S IDEA OF HAPPINESS

We can think of normative ethical theory from two moral perspectives: The perspective of action and the perspective of character. Aristotle's emphasis is on the question of character. His fundamental concern is to show how the cultivation of the virtues in us conduces to a flourishing, happy life. In order to do this, Aristotle views ethical theory in the larger context of a conception of human nature, one that seeks to identify the proper function and purpose of being human. According to Aristotle, everything aims at some goal, has some purpose. Natural things have this purpose built-in and function in such a way so as to realize their ends. In order to lead a moral life, we need to understand what that purpose is for us and to determine the best means for achieving it.

Aristotle's theory is a prime example of *teleology* (from the Greek *telos,* meaning purpose). A teleological conception of nature says that everything has a good at which it aims and in order to achieve that good, it exercises a function that is proper to the kind of thing it is. The goal of human nature, according to Aristotle, is happiness, where this is understood not simply as a particular conscious state or feeling, but as general well-being or the quality of a flourishing life. Happiness, in this sense, is lifelong pursuit accomplished by exercising the proper function of being human. Aristotle arrives at a notion of what constitutes our proper function by considering how we understand other kinds of things. For instance: Artists, musicians, and carpenters have functions; the various parts of the body—the eye, the heart, the kidneys, the lungs—each have a function. Wouldn't it be odd to assume that all these things have a function, but a human being does not? The function of a human being should be something particular to human beings. It cannot be just life, because all other living things have that. It cannot be sensation, because that is shared by animals. What distinguishes human beings from other living things is the capacity to reason, and it is in terms of the use of reason that we are directed toward happiness as a goal.

According to Aristotle, happiness is our greatest good, that which we desire for its own sake, and we desire all other goods in order to ultimately attain happiness. But what is happiness? Aristotle considers some common conceptions, or misconceptions, like happiness is pleasure, or honor, or wealth. The goal of anything is necessarily related to its proper function; if the proper function of being human is to be rational, then happiness is possible only for a being capable of reason. It should be evident then why Aristotle rejects the idea that happiness is the same thing as pleasure. Pleasure is not unique to humans. Animals with a high level of sentience are capable of feeling pleasure. Moreover, pleasure is a momentary sensation. It is there only as long as one experiences the feeling. Happiness is not just a momentary sensation or even a collection of good feelings, but rather "an activity of the soul"—as Aristotle calls it—in accordance with our rational capacity to develop the virtues. Happiness is not honor. Honor depends on what others think of us, and while it matters how others view us, this would be too superficial a notion of happiness. We pursue honor and wish to be viewed positively by others in order to reassure ourselves that we are good in some sense. So honor is not pursued for its own sake. For the same reason, wealth is not happiness, since we pursue wealth for the sake of something else.

In suggesting that happiness is "an activity of the soul" Aristotle doesn't mean to say that other goods, like pleasure, or honor, or wealth, aren't of value at all. On the contrary, he includes them in his analysis of a flourishing life precisely because it is hard to imagine how one can be happy if one suffers pain, has a bad reputation, and live in poverty. In this way his notion of happiness combines the teleological concept of proper function with the common sense idea that the material conditions of one's life make it difficult to attain happiness. At the same time, he believes that the virtuous person is best able to deal with adversity and the contingencies of life.

Happiness also consists in balancing reason and emotion. The emotions are not just unbridled desires that need to be reined in or suppressed by reason. Instead they can be imbued with rationality in the sense that we can develop an understanding of when and to what extent we should exhibit and act on our emotions. The moral life is lived not in isolation but with others, and the point of ethics is to enable us to live well with others. Our relationships with others in a moral community are wide and varied and involve the entire range of human capacities, not simply an intellectual awareness of what is right and wrong.

As with anything, human beings can function well or poorly. Happiness, in so far as it is an activity of our fundamental nature, is what it means for us to function well. It is the development, possession, and exercise of the virtues that constitutes the essential core of happiness. Only the virtuous person, the person with a firm and fixed good character, can attain happiness. The virtues, then, benefit those who have them and account for why the virtuous person can be said, in some sense, to have attained fulfillment even in the face of adversity and just plain bad luck. It is the vicious person that is truly miserable.

When Aristotle says that we are rational by nature he means that the power to reason is our distinctive function, but it is important to note that rationality is not simply a disposition that directs us toward knowledge and theoretical understanding. From the moral perspective, rationality is fundamentally an activity that, when exercised well, also leads us to frame the virtues for ourselves. The practical function of reason is to get us to live well in the world. Certainly this involves a kind of knowledge and understanding, an exercise of what Aristotle calls the "intellectual virtues," but living well in the world involves more than just knowing things. It also involves acting and feeling, and these too can be done well or poorly.

The achievement of a well-functioning life is accomplished through what Aristotle calls "practical wisdom" (*phronesis*). Think of it this way: To live well in the world, we don't just require an abstract understanding of what is right and wrong. We need to know what to do and how to direct our actions in particular situations—what to do when, what feelings to have and to what extent, what people are affected by our actions, and so on. So practical wisdom is an organizing activity, a special ability that aims at striking the right balance in action and feeling.

ARISTOTLE'S THEORY OF VIRTUE

What are the virtues specifically and how is it that we have them at all? In the first instance, Aristotle says that the virtues are not in us by nature; we need to acquire them. We do have a natural capacity to acquire the virtues; that is the function of reason, but character is formed over time. The virtues are formed in us through habit. That is, we learn to be virtuous by practicing those actions that virtuous persons perform. This is the reason Aristotle claims that the virtues are not in us by nature: What is natural cannot be changed through habit. Natural capacities are innate and not acquired through habituation. We can come to be virtuous, to develop traits that go to constitute character. If the virtues were already in us by nature, there would be neither a need nor a way to acquire or change them. The idea of habituation is important here because it indicates that the virtues cannot be taught or learned in a purely intellectual way. Think analogously of learning to play a musical instrument; you can read all you want about it, but the only way to learn to play the guitar, for instance, is through practice. It is likewise with virtues such as courage or generosity. We can only come to be courageous or generous by persistently practicing courageous or generous acts.

Just as the virtues are formed through habit, so are the vices. If the virtues are formed through good habits, then the vices are formed through bad habits. You play the guitar, perhaps, but play it badly. Maybe you've developed bad habits with respect to certain mechanics, holding the instrument wrong, or fingering chords improperly; or maybe you fail in listening sufficiently to intonation and frequently play out of tune, etc. If these become ingrained, you will continue to play the guitar badly. It could change, of course, in that you might become a better guitar player, but not mystically or magically. You'd have to undo the bad habits (something which could be exceedingly difficult) and develop good ones. Here again it is likewise with the vices. If a person persistently acts in miserly or stingy ways and gets in the habit of doing so, then he or she will become a stingy person. To do so is to act less than reasonably or in accordance with our best nature. As a result one forms a bad character. To act in accordance with our rational nature, to practice good ways of behaving, will lead to the cultivation of a good character.

There is nonetheless an important difference between performing actions that we might call virtuous and actually being virtuous. Aristotle addresses this issue by first considering a puzzle about virtue, one that initially appears as a paradox. How can we become good, if we are not already good? Consider these two propositions:

1. To be virtuous, a person must perform virtuous acts.
2. In order to perform virtuous acts, one must already be virtuous.

If performing generous actions, for instance, requires that a person have a generous character, then that seems to violate the idea that we develop character only through practice and habit. But if a person develops a generous character only by acting generously, then that seems to violate the idea that only a generous person can act generously. This seems to imply that a person can be generous before he or she has developed a generous character. But that's precisely what Aristotle denies is possible, since virtues are not in us by nature but are learned through habit.

Aristotle's way of solving this puzzle is ingenious. He says that actions may conform to virtue but not yet be virtuous. Think of it adverbially: In order for an action to be virtuous it must be performed virtuously. That is, actions are virtuous when they are performed in the manner in which a virtuous person performs them. Most generally, this means that actions are virtuous when they are performed reasonably, in accordance with our best rational nature; but this doesn't say much. What precisely is the manner in which virtuous persons perform their actions? Aristotle specifies the conditions of acting virtuously by noting certain characteristics of the virtuous person. These are:

1. The virtuous person *knows* that a particular action is virtuous and understands why it is the right thing to do in a particular circumstance.
2. The virtuous person *decides* to perform the action and freely chooses to do so. In this sense, the virtuous person is motivated by his character and intends to perform an action because of it is judged to coincide with virtue.
3. The virtuous person acts from a *firm and unchanging state* and on the basis of habit has cultivated a good character.

In examining these requirements for virtuous actions, we can see the integral connection between a person's character and what a person does. That is, we can see the specific ways in which one's actions accord with reason.

Notice also that we can see how an action conforms to virtue but does not yet count as virtuous. Consider what and how we teach our children. A mother says to her six-year-old son, "Share your toys with your sister." The little boy does what his mother says, but he doesn't *know* why his action is good and is *motivated* not by the characteristic of the act itself, but perhaps by the avoidance of punishment or the expectation of a reward. He is simply following Mom's orders and does not freely *decide* to do it, and certainly doesn't act from a *firm and unchanging state* as he is just beginning to learn good habits and does not yet have a fully developed character.

This example demonstrates not only how we come to learn the virtues but also how important it is to have proper guidance in life. Moral education is not like theoretical learning; it can't be gotten by studying or reading a manual. Learning to be virtuous depends on living in a social environment—a family say—where there are those who serve as moral exemplars for us. The example also highlights the fact that without such guidance and in the absence of those who serve as moral exemplars, a person is at a distinct liability in that it becomes exceedingly difficult to learn those habits of acting that lead to the development of good character. Matters are even worse when those who guide others are themselves persons of bad character.

The virtuous person, then, is one who exercises practical wisdom and who understands the connection between reason and virtue and who knows the right thing to do in what circumstances. But just what is a virtue? Aristotle says that a virtue is an intermediate or mean between two extremes, one of excess and one of deficiency. He writes:

Both excessive and defective exercise destroys the strength, and similarly drink or food which is above or below a certain amount destroys the health, while that which is proportionate both produces and increases and preserves it. So too is it, then, in the case of temperance and courage and the other virtues. The man who runs away from everything in fear, and faces up to nothing, becomes a coward; the man who is absolutely fearless, and will walk into anything, becomes rash. It is the same with the man who gets enjoyment from all the pleasures, abstaining from none: he is immoderate; whereas he who avoids all pleasures, like a boor, is a man of no sensitivity[2]

In acting virtuously, we try to strike a proper balance; there should never be too much excess or too much deficiency when it comes to the virtues. It is the extremes that damage people. For instance, a person who eats too much or eats too little will not be healthy. Similarly for the "soul," a person who acts in an extreme manner will not be virtuous. A virtue then is a state of character that exemplifies a balance between some form of excessiveness, on the one hand, and some form of deficiency, on the other. So the courageous person for example, is one who is neither excessively fearful nor rash or foolhardy. Think of this in ordinary terms. It is likely that you have encountered individuals who are incapable of dealing with even the most minimal kind of adversity; they seem to be paralyzed by fear. Then there are those who take unnecessary and foolish risks, who put themselves and others in jeopardy by doing so. Or perhaps you know a person with virtually no sense of humor at all, one who takes even the lightest of situations as an occasion for the deepest of reflections or a person who shows up at a serious occasion wearing a bulbous nose and slap shoes. Or maybe one of your friends is a sheer pleasure seeker and another seemingly devoid of any capacity to enjoy herself. You might have been embarrassed by a relative's extravagance in giving gifts or appalled by someone's stinginess. The story is the same in each case: Somewhere between the extremes is a properly balanced action.

This proper balance is what is sometimes called the "golden mean." The virtuous person effects this mean by doing the right thing, at the right time, and with the right aim. This applies not only straightforwardly to actions, but also to emotions, which have profound bearing on our relationships with others. Consider anger as an example. There are many occasions when we get angry without any real justification. Aristotle says it's easy to just get angry, anyone can do that. It is difficult, however, to manifest anger in a properly balanced (virtuous) way. It is difficult to be angry with the right person, to the right extent, at the right time, in the right way, with the right aim. This calls attention to just how hard it is to be virtuous and why developing a virtuous character is such a fine accomplishment. He writes:

… it is no easy task to be good. For in everything it is no easy task to find the middle, e.g. to find the middle of a circle is not for everyone but for him who knows; so, too, any one can get angry—that is easy—or give or spend money; but to do this to the right person, to the right extent, at the right time, with the right motive, and in the right way, that is not for everyone, nor is it easy; wherefore goodness is both rare and laudable and noble.[3]

Aristotle recognizes that the notion that a virtue is a mean between extremes needs further clarification. There are three factors to consider in this regard. First, it should be understood that not every action or emotion has a mean. There can be no golden mean of actions like adultery. Consider an adulterer who attempts to justify his actions by saying he didn't commit too much adultery or too little, but given the circumstances just the right amount. He committed adultery with the right person, to the right extent, at the right time, in the right way, with the right aim. That would be preposterous. This is also the case with certain emotions, which by their nature are destructive. Take envy for instance—envy is the feeling of being pained by the good fortune of others. Is there ever a properly balanced way to express that emotion in a moral context? Some actions and emotions are wrong because they are already extremes, already deficiencies and so could not conduce to one's happiness and, in fact, are destructive to those who perform such actions or cultivate such emotions. No extreme could ever qualify as a virtuous character.

Second, Aristotle says the mean is "relative to us." There is no one position that is the intermediate for every person; the mean is not the same for everyone. For some people going into a burning building would be reckless, for others it would be appropriate and courageous. If one has asthma and is frail, then it would be foolish to attempt a daring rescue in a burning building; but for a trained firefighter with appropriate strength and skill it would be a courageous act. We wouldn't think that the asthmatic is a coward for not running into the burning building, though we might think that a firefighter that refused to do is weak in virtue. Likewise while we think it would be reckless for the asthmatic to run into the burning building, we wouldn't think that the firefighter is reckless for doing so. The mean is the appropriate way of acting given our individual strengths and weaknesses and the particular circumstances in which we are called upon to act. Recklessness and cowardice are both vices in that they are extremes that involve, in this case, too little or too much fear. No extreme can be measured in a rational way. In this sense, no extreme can ever count as a virtue. This is another way of understanding why it is difficult to fix on the mean. There is no formula for doing so. Instead we need to employ a wealth of knowledge in making a determination of how to act. We need to know our own states of character, our particular strengths and weaknesses, and our own inclinations. We need to know who will be affected by our actions and what the circumstances are. This requires that we put our reason to use and exercise the practical wisdom required to function well. It may be that certain states of character are so firmly fixed in us that they become "second nature," but even with this it is impossible to predict all that life might throw our way. Practical wisdom and a well-developed character are the best means available to deal with whatever contingencies may arise.

Third, following from the idea that the mean is "relative to us" and in the absence of a general formula for determining an exact mean that applies to all persons in all circumstances, Aristotle proposes three general guiding principles that, when applied, give us the best chance of hitting the mean. These are:

1. Avoid that extreme that is more opposed to the mean.
2. Avoid the easier extreme.
3. Be careful with pleasure.

One extreme is more opposed to the other. Let's stick with courage as an example. Courage is more like rash behavior in that it requires a diminished sense of fear. In this regard, cowardice is the extreme more opposed to the mean. So we should avoid being overly fearful. Generosity is closer to extravagance than to miserliness, so avoid being stingy. But we also need to take account of individual tendencies, and so some person might find it easier to be rash and reckless. In that case, the easier extreme should be avoided. Pleasure poses a particularly difficult problem for us. There is nothing wrong in feeling pleasure, in fact we become insensitive if we try to avoid it altogether. A little reflection demonstrates, however, that the difficulty emerges because it is initially seems so natural to feel pleasure at the extremes. So the macho man feels pleasure in his daredevil behavior, the coward in knowing that he wasn't at any risk, the glutton in overeating, the cigarette smoker in her nicotine fix, and the promiscuous person in self-indulgent, profligate sex. To such individuals, even the mean seems painful. But if practical reason can lead to a moderation of behavior and the development of habits that cultivate better states of character, then we could conceivably learn to take pleasure in being virtuous.

SOME FINAL THOUGHTS

There are several criticisms of virtue theory that bring us back to many of the issues examined throughout this text. A common argument against virtue ethics is that it is insufficiently normative or action-guiding; it does not provide a set of rules for determining what actions are right or wrong. At least, utilitarianism and Kantian deontology give criteria for deciding what actions are right or wrong. The virtue theorist might respond that action is guided not so much by rules or principles as it is guided by character, and since there is no one way to be a person of good character, different actions may be required of different individuals. The fundamental point of ethics is to aid, then, in the cultivation of those states that lead to good actions.

In a related way, some criticize virtue theory because it relies too heavily on the contingencies of human life and the notion of moral luck. Other normative theories try, at least, to minimize the role of luck (utilitarianism) or eliminate it altogether (deontology). If we are to hold people responsible for their actions, to praise or blame them for their actions, then there must be a clear and objective basis on which to make such judgments. Virtue theory recognizes, however, that it is just a fact that the circumstances of life are beyond our control. Some people are lucky enough to have proper guidance and good moral exemplars that aid in the development of good character, while others are at a liability because they lack that guidance and are confronted with only bad influences. But such factors alone do not completely determine how one turns out. As Aristotle himself suggested, the virtues best equip us to deal with adversity. Developing the virtues and sustaining them is difficult under any circumstance; we are all vulnerable to life's contingencies and any goodness we achieve is itself fragile. This is an "essential feature of the human condition, which makes the attainment of the good life all the more valuable."[4]

Some say that virtue ethics is just a fancy form of egoism in that it focuses on oneself and emphasizes how one benefits from having the virtues. One who holds this view might argue further that if the goal is happiness, then all my actions are in some sense directed toward my ultimate interest. But this seems to miss the point about happiness. It's not that we act just so that we feel happy, but rather that our well-being depends on how well we exercise practical judgment in developing a character that enables us to live well with others. The virtues, then, are not just self-directed, in having them a person performs actions that necessarily benefit others. There is no contradiction in also saying that the virtues benefit those who possess them.

Others argue that virtue ethics implies relativism. Aristotle's own theory, they might suggest, is suitable for a Greek aristocrat, but some other culture may value other virtues. This too is to miss a salient feature of the idea of virtue. Namely that the goal of ethics is to lead a moral life in a community, to live well with others, and though there may be some variability in how that is accomplished, it can't be that we could function well in a moral community without any conception of virtues like justice, truthfulness, generosity, courage, and friendliness. Some virtues are requirements for any human being to lead a flourishing life. In addition, the relativist denies that there is an objective human nature. Virtue theory requires that a general human capacity, reason, if you will, be put to practical use in determining how best to live in the circumstances in which one finds oneself. The application of the virtues may indeed be "context-sensitive," but that there are virtues at all is not.[5]

Virtue theory may have an advantage over other normative ethical theories in so far as it recognizes that we cannot separate morality from the world as we find it, that we cannot act in isolation from those with whom we actually live, that we cannot exclude desires from our pursuit of moral goodness, and that we have not succeeded in living well by just following rules and doing good things. If character is source of action, then it matters what kind of persons we are.

ENDNOTES

1. This chapter provides a brief summary of some central ideas in Aristotle's *Nichomachean Ethics*. Specifically, it focuses on the idea of happiness, the theory that virtue is a "mean between extremes," and the idea of virtue as a state of character. There are numerous translations of this work; a particularly readable one is: *The Nichomachean Ethics*, translated by W. D. Ross (Oxford University Press, 1959). References here are to that translation.
2. Aristotle, *Nichomachean Ethics*, Book II, chapter 2.
3. Aristotle, *Nichomachean Ethics*, Book II, chapter 9.
4. See the entry on virtue ethics by Nafsika Athanassoulis in the Internet Encyclopedia of Philosophy (http://www.iep.utm.edu/virtue/).
5. See Martha C. Nussbaum, "Non-Relative Virtues: An Aristotelian Approach," in *The Quality of Life*, edited by Martha C. Nussbaum and Amartya Sen, (Oxford University Press, 1993) pp. 242–70.

STUDY QUESTIONS

6. How does virtue ethics differ from consequentialism and deontology?

7. What is *teleology*? In what sense is Aristotle's virtue ethics *teleological*?

8. Explain Aristotle's conception of happiness. How is happiness different from pleasure?

9. What is the fundamental difference between "intellectual virtues" and "moral virtues"? What is "practical wisdom"?

10. Aristotle argues that the virtues are not in us by nature. How so? How, according to Aristotle, do we acquire the virtues?

11. What puzzle about virtue does Aristotle present? What is his solution?

12. What does it mean to say that "an action is virtuous when it is performed virtuously"? What is the manner in which a virtuous person acts?

13. Explain the idea that virtue is a mean between extremes. What is the "golden mean"? Aristotle says that the mean is "relative to us." Explain that idea and think of some examples of your own.

14. Though there is no exact way to hit the mean, Aristotle provides several general guidelines. What are they?

QUESTIONS FOR REFLECTION

1. Is morality primarily about performing right actions or being good persons?

2. Do you think it is difficult to be virtuous?

3. How might the virtues benefit those who possess them? What has character got to do with happiness?

4. Aristotle's conception of the virtues is grounded in the idea that human beings have an essential function. Do you think we have such a function? Is happiness our purpose?

SUGGESTIONS FOR FURTHER READING

Anscombe, G. E. M. "Modern Moral Philosophy," *Philosophy*: 33, 1958.

Bennett, Jonathan. "The Conscience of Huckleberry Finn," *Philosophy*: 49, 1974.

Foot, Philippa. *Virtues and Vices*. Oxford: Blackwell, 1978.

Hursthouse, Rosalind. *On Virtue Ethics*. Oxford: Oxford University Press, 1999.

MacIntyre, Alasdair. *After Virtue*. London: Duckworth, 1985.

Mayo, Bernard. *Ethics and the Moral Life*. New York: St. Martin's Press, 1958.

Murdoch, Iris. *The Sovereignty of Good*. London: Ark, 1985.

Nussbaum, Martha C. "Virtue Ethics: A Misleading Category?" *Journal of Ethics:* 3, 1999.

Shklar, Judith N. *Ordinary Vices*. Cambridge, MA: Harvard University Press, 1984.

Taylor, Gabriele. *Deadly Vices*. Oxford: Oxford University Press, 2006.

CHAPTER 8
Utilitarianism

Utilitarianism, as discussed in the previous chapter, is rooted in a theory of value. It seeks to identify in the first instance, what counts as good for us. Jeremy Bentham and John Stuart Mill, despite the respective differences in their views regarding the quantitative or qualitative approach to pleasure, are both hedonists in that they argue that pleasure and pleasure alone is desirable as an end in itself. It was also noted in the discussion that utilitarianism is the kind of normative ethical theory called *consequentialism*—a theory of right conduct that determines the rightness or wrongness of actions in terms of outcomes or consequences of actions. For the utilitarian, the concept of the good and the idea that consequences determine moral rightness and wrongness go hand-in-hand. The goal of moral action is to bring about the good, not just for oneself but for the greatest number. For the hedonistic utilitarians, then, pleasure has intrinsic value and is worth pursuing, and moral action should maximize pleasure (or at the very least minimize pain) for the greatest number of those affected by an action. As a consequentialist theory, utilitarianism says that an action is morally right when it succeeds in maximizing the good (or minimizing the bad if that's the best alternative) and wrong when it fails to do so. In short, utilitarianism says that what is morally right depends on a prior notion of what is intrinsically good. The focus of the previous chapter was on the concept of the good; the emphasis in this chapter is on utilitarianism as a theory of right conduct, and so the focus is on the concept of consequences as the criterion for morally correct action.

Utilitarianism has a rather elegantly simple conception of the purpose of morality. The point of moral action is to produce a circumstance where more people are made better off, where the good is distributed in such a way that a maximum number of people benefit from our actions. In this way, the utilitarian understands morality fundamentally as a way of improving the world. This is a way of understanding, in the most general terms possible, the point of consequentialism. What matters is the circumstance produced by actions, not the intentions behind our actions or even whether an action consists with a common sense view of morality that might involve concepts like rules, rights, and obligations. For the utilitarian, the only rule of morality is to perform actions that result in maximizing the overall good in the world.

Let's consider consequentialism a bit more precisely. Utilitarian theory holds that the evaluation of actions is determined exclusively in terms of the consequences they produce; the morality of an action is determined solely through an assessment of its consequences and nothing else. Our only obligation or duty in any situation is to perform that action, from among the alternative courses of action, which will result in the greatest possible balance of good over evil. Notice that this is an obligation or duty in the most abstract sense in that it really doesn't say which specific actions are right or wrong but only how it is that any action is right or wrong.

The right thing to do, in any situation, is whatever would produce the best overall outcome for all those who will be affected by your action. The morally right action, the one we ought to perform, is the one that produces the best overall consequences for everyone.

What's important in utilitarian consequentialism is not necessarily who enjoys the benefits, but only that the net outcome is positive. Each person's benefit is equally important, so what matters is the overall good that is produced. Despite the apparent simplicity of the utilitarian approach, it actually requires a great deal of moral effort to achieve the goal of maximizing benefit. Utilitarianism requires that we always do the most we can to ensure that the good is distributed in such a way that the greatest number benefit. This makes morality a strenuous exercise, as we should never be content with only having done the minimum. Moreover, it requires that we set aside our own interests and the interests of those close to us and view ourselves and **all** others (not just those close to us) as equal in the capacity to be beneficiaries of moral action.

It is important also to see just what is excluded in the consequentialist's analysis of the morality of actions. To say that the overall good produced by an action is the exclusive determinant of an action's rightness or wrongness, is to deny any value to other concepts that typically play a role in our common sense notion of morality, concepts like intention, duty, the intrinsic worth of an action, or even one's character. From the consequentialist perspective, intentions are irrelevant in moral assessments. An action could very well have positive or negative unintended consequences and the action would be deemed right or wrong irrespective of what was intended in performing it. It also wouldn't make sense to say that an action is right or wrong in and of itself or that we have a duty to perform or refrain from performing certain actions independently of the outcomes of those actions, since that would be to exclude consequences from our moral assessments. In this respect, consequentialism is distinguished from duty ethics or *deontology*. It is also distinguished from *virtue ethics,* which emphasizes the moral qualities a person cultivates in himself or herself. A person's character doesn't matter to the consequentialist in that one does not have to be a virtuous person, or any sort of person in particular for that matter, to perform actions that wind up having good results. Whether it's likely that a person of bad character or with bad intentions will consistently perform actions with overall positive consequences is another matter. What is important here is that it is simply possible for such a person to do so. As we will see, such exclusions form the basis of some serious criticisms of utilitarianism.

In so far as it provides what it takes to be an objective and person-neutral criterion for the determination of moral rightness and wrongness, utilitarianism conceives of moral theory as kind of "science" of action. All we need do to meet the demands of the theory is to determine, from among all possible courses of action we could take, that action that will have the greatest overall positive outcome. Assuming people agree that the purpose of morality is, in fact, to produce optimific results and improve the circumstances in the world, utilitarianism employs a decision procedure that leads to ethical conclusions, free of subjective interests and which, when viewed in light of objective criteria, should settle our moral disagreements. Is it possible to arrive at the kind of certainty about outcomes that utilitarian theory seems to demand? And, even if it were possible to do so, would we have succeeded in explaining the moral life? Is morality simply about actions and consequences? What, if anything, might a moral theory have to say about intentions, obligations, and character?

UTILITARIAN DECISION-MAKING

Recall Bentham's quantitative hedonism and his idea that it is possible to ascribe numerical values to pleasure and pain states according to certain criteria: *Intensity, duration, certainty, propinquity, fecundity, purity,* and *extent.* With respect to determining the utility of an action—its tendency to produce good consequences—and hence which course of action we should take, Bentham recommends the following procedure: Imagine that an action affects a certain number of persons (the extent) whose interests are concerned. For each individual affected by an action compute a value for each pleasure and pain in terms of each criterion—how deeply felt, how long lasting, how near or remote, how likely to produce sensations of the same sort or opposite sort, etc. Then sum up the value of each pleasure and sum up the value of each pain for each individual; if the sum of pleasure is greater, then the action has positive utility for an individual; if the sum of pain is greater than that of pleasure, then the action has negative utility for an individual. Once done for each individual, then sum up the numbers representing those who are positively affected and the numbers representing those negatively affected. This will give the utility of an action in terms of how it affects an entire community of individuals—the good tendency of the act is determined by a positive net balance of pleasure over pain; the bad tendency of an act is determined by a net balance of pain over pleasure. The moral demand: Perform that action which has the greatest net positive balance of pleasure (good) over pain (evil).[1]

Is it really conceivable that we should be required to employ this kind of analysis prior to making a moral judgment or ethical decision to act? By the time the process were complete and future results predicted, with no guarantee that they will occur, the need to act at all might have long passed. Bentham anticipates such concerns when he writes that:

> *It is not to be expected that this process be strictly pursued previously to every moral judgment … It may, however, be always kept in view: and as near as the process actually pursued on these occasions approaches to it, so near will such process approach to the character of an exact one.*[2]

How do or can we even know precisely how other individuals will be affected by our actions? Shouldn't morality be grounded on surer footing than the possibility or presumed likelihood of future outcomes? Is it even desirable at all to think of moral theory as an "exact science"? Wouldn't we be paralyzed by the process and perhaps cause greater harm in not acting as a result?

The issue is further complicated when we consider Mill's conception of qualitatively better forms of pleasure, as it is impossible to measure such pleasure in terms of magnitudes. But even if we reject the quantitative approach and the algorithmic decision procedure that attends it, we might still adopt the kind of heuristic contained in the quote from Bentham above. That is, while it is hardly likely that we could think of every possible consequence an action would have for an entire population of individuals, we should consider how they could conceivably be affected by our actions. We may have an intuitive sense about minimizing suffering and become more acutely aware of employing the utilitarian criterion of rightness with developed experience of acting in the world.

Take, for example, a simple version of the famous thought experiment called the *trolley problem*.[3] A trolley is barreling down a track out of control. On the track ahead in direct line of the runaway trolley are four workers who will be unable to get out of the way by the time the trolley reaches their position. All four will certainly be killed if the trolley hits them. There is, however, a switch that will divert the trolley onto a side track. You are standing at the switch and realize you can divert the trolley by flipping the switch. You also notice that there is a single individual on the side track who will certainly be killed if the trolley is diverted. Given this circumstance, should you pull the switch?

Many people, without much hesitation, say that the right thing to do is to pull the switch and divert the trolley even with the knowledge that one person will certainly be killed. Why so? In the first place, it seems to involve a simple calculation: The death of four people is worse than the death of one. But there's more to it. If you could prevent the worse outcome, then you ought to do so. Moreover, you ought to do so even though you are not directly responsible for what happens as a result of the trolley running out of control and even in knowing that the death of the person on the side track is the direct result of an action (flipping the switch) you took. There is not enough time to apply the utilitarian calculus in this case, even with such a small population to consider, but, as Bentham suggests, it is "kept in view." The situation, particularly the experience you have of being at the switch, triggers the moral intuition about minimizing suffering and the utilitarian criterion of rightness provides a justification for pulling the switch and diverting the trolley towards a single individual. Again what matters is the positive outcome, in this case fewer dead people.

But is the outcome really the only thing that matters? Does it matter, for instance, how it is that the people in the trolley example would come to be killed? If you pull the switch, then you have aimed the trolley at a single individual and thus would have killed that person. This is not necessarily to make a moral judgment, rather simply to state a fact. If you don't pull the switch, then you would have killed no one, but you would have let four people die. That said, there may be a moral difference between killing and letting die. If we go by the numbers alone, it seems that it is simply worse to let four die than to kill one. If, however, we believe that killing one may be worse than letting four people die, then something other than outcomes would matter in our moral decision making. One might hold to a moral principle like "killing is wrong" and believe that we ought not to perform wrong actions even to bring out good consequences. Perhaps changes in the circumstances may lead to shifting judgments even given the same net outcome.

Consider the same trolley scenario but suppose there was no switch and you could stop the trolley by pushing a person in front of it; or you could stop the trolley by jumping in front of it yourself—in either case, the other person or you will die and the four workers will not be killed. Should you push the person? Should you jump? Is there really any difference between pulling a switch and aiming a trolley at a person or pushing a person in front of a trolley if the outcome is the same? And if the outcome is all that matters shouldn't you jump in front of the trolley? Remember from the utilitarian perspective everyone's interests count equally. Or imagine the exact same scenario but with this difference: The single individual on the side track happens to be your aunt, whom you love dearly. Should it make any difference that the person on the side track is a family member? Should your emotional attachment to that person be a factor? Do you have special obligations to family members that must factor alongside any consideration of consequences?

In keeping the outcome the same while shifting the circumstances, we begin to see that there are problems with utilitarianism, even in a case where a simple calculation or intuition initially produced what appeared to be an obvious solution to the problem. This calls into question the universal applicability of the utilitarian criterion of moral rightness. There is at least a tension in the effort to apply utilitarian decision making across the board. In response to this, some utilitarians retrench and reaffirm the idea that consequences are all that matter; others attempt to temper the tension by introducing rules into the mix.

ACT-UTILITARIANISM AND RULE-UTILITARIANISM

It is standard practice to distinguish between two fundamental forms of utilitarianism, *act- utilitarianism* and *rule-utilitarianism*. Since these are both forms of utilitarianism, there is a common element in them. Both are consequentialist theories in that they hold the idea that moral rightness and wrongness are determined by outcomes and both accept the view that the purpose of morality is to improve the circumstances in the world, to bring about the greatest good for the greatest number. They differ significantly in terms of what counts when determining the consequences of actions. Begin with these basic definitions:

Act-utilitarianism is the view that an action is right or wrong based **solely** on the consequences of that action itself.
Rule-utilitarianism is the view that an action is right or wrong depending on whether it conforms to a general moral rule, obedience to which tends to bring about good consequences.

Act-utilitarianism is a pure form of utilitarianism. It denies that there is any way to determine the morality of actions independently of consequences. Each act is taken on its own and in its own situation. Except for the imperative to perform actions that, as far as we can reasonably predict, will produce optimal outcomes, there is no need to introduce general moral rules that range over classes of actions irrespective of the situation in which an action is performed. In effect, act utilitarianism says that the best chance we have to improve the general circumstances of the world is to consider each act individually. If we perform actions in each situation that bring about the best overall consequences and then add all those consequences together, it follows from the act-utilitarian perspective that we will have made the world a better place.

Rule-utilitarianism adopts the view that general moral rules must play a role in the determination of consequences. A particular action is viewed not solely in the context of its situation but in terms of whether it adheres to a general moral rule (e.g., always keep your promises). The moral rule itself, however, is not isolated from consequences; its value precisely as a rule is measured by the fact that, in general, obedience to the rule is the best way of assuring that good outcomes are produced. In this way, rule-utilitarianism is a theory that combines the core idea of consequentialism with a deontological element—the idea that we have certain moral obligations that obtain irrespective of any particular situation in which we may find ourselves.

Act-utilitarians argue that rule-utilitarianism is incoherent. Consider what happens in a situation where obedience to a rule conflicts with bringing about the best overall consequences. What should a rule-utilitarian do in that circumstance? Follow the rule or bring about good consequences? If rule-utilitarianism says that we should still follow the rule even though the best overall consequences in that situation would not result, then this would be to undermine the consequentialist aspect of the theory. It's hard to see how this counts as utilitarianism any longer. Does it help to respond, as a rule-utilitarian might, that it's not each specific application of a rule that matters but that, in general, obedience to the rule brings about the best consequences?

So even in the case of conflict between the rule and consequences, it is best to obey the rule because the world is better if most people do so. The act-utilitarian argues that this still violates the fundamental principle of utilitarianism that in each case where we are to act we should strive to generate the best overall consequences. In settling the rule-consequences conflict this way, the rule-utilitarian values rules more than consequences. What if the conflict is settled on the side of consequences? A rule-utilitarian could argue that some particular situation is exactly the sort that requires us to make an exception to a rule. We might even amend the rule and say, "always obey the rule, except in situations like … ." In this case, the rule-utilitarian is opting for consequences over the rule. The act-utilitarian argues that it is practically impossible to foresee all such instances where exceptions would be allowed, and so it would not be possible to build all exceptions into a general rule. The rule would die the death of a thousand exceptions. If that's the case, then we should just go with act-utilitarianism and let the situation dictate.

In sum, act-utilitarianism argues that rule-utilitarianism is either a form of duty ethics, in which case it is inconsistent with consequentialism or it simply reduces to act-utilitarianism by opting for consequences over rules in specific situations. From this perspective, it seems that the only consistent and coherent form of utilitarianism is act-utilitarianism.[4]

But is this really the final word? Does act-utilitarianism fare any better as a moral theory than rule-utilitarianism? Let's consider two cases of the sort philosophers commonly construct that might shed further light on the matter:

The case of the deathbed promise: *Your grandfather, a very wealthy man, has named you in his will and you stand to inherit ten million dollars when he dies. He is a strong supporter of second amendment rights and a generous contributor to the National Rifle Association. With no time to change his will, on his deathbed, he asks you to promise that you will contribute one million dollars to the NRA upon receiving your inheritance. You make the promise; your grandfather dies. You are not especially in favor of the NRA, and when you receive your inheritance, you determine that the money could be put to better use by donating it to the Save the Children Fund, helping children in developing countries. What should you do, keep your promise or do more good by helping children?*

The case of the unwitting homeless organ donor: *A homeless man enters a hospital emergency room to have a cut on his leg stitched and treated. Upon examination, the attending doctor finds the man completely healthy. In the hospital are three people waiting for transplants, one needs a kidney, one a heart, and one a lung; they will die soon if they do not receive donor organs. It just so happens that the homeless man is a match for all three. The doctor decides that he should kill the homeless man, remove his organs, and save the three transplant patients. After all, he reasons, think of the good consequences, the three patients will survive and enjoy their lives, their families will be happy, and besides no one would even notice that the homeless man was gone. Did the doctor do the morally right thing?*

Factoring consequences alone, the act-utilitarian has pat answers in both cases: Break your promise and kill one to save three. This presents a difficulty for act-utilitarianism in that the theory seemingly allows for actions which are wrong from a straightforward common conception of morality, which includes moral convictions like it is right to keep your promises (however uncomfortable it might be to do so) and wrong to kill the innocent (even if good consequences result from the act). In certain cases, then, act-utilitarianism would require us to perform actions that violate our firmly held moral beliefs. Should we just "bite the bullet," as the expression goes, and sacrifice our convictions for end results?

Now it looks as if rule-utilitarianism might provide the better responses in these two situations. It asks us to consider what the consequences would be if everyone decided not to keep promises when it was uncomfortable to do so or if doctors routinely killed unwitting homeless people to save the lives of others. Though this line of reasoning has the benefit of being more consistent with our ordinary moral conceptions, it still may not yet be sufficient in terms of justifying why we hold our moral rules to be valuable. Perhaps there are more fundamental reasons why we value moral rules. In the case of promise keeping, for instance, it could be that we simply owe it to others to do what the promise says we will do; or that keeping promises is a form of honesty and we value honesty; or, pertaining to the case above, that we view a deathbed promise as a solemn vow, or that we have unique obligations to our grandparents. We might believe that it is wrong to kill the innocent not because of the consequences that might be produced if it became a general practice, but because a person has a right to his or life.

The point here is that the reasons for valuing and following moral rules could be construed as independent of the outcomes of acting according to those rules. The issue is not only about choosing one form of utilitarianism over another, but rather whether any form of utilitarianism is adequate as a moral theory. We turn now to some criticisms of utilitarianism.

SOME CRITICISMS OF UTILITARIANISM

Throughout the preceding remarks, there are indications of serious flaws in utilitarian theory. As we have seen, utilitarianism, in so far as it is a form of consequentialism, makes right action parasitic on a prior concept of the good. In this way what is right is most generally understood as the means to bring about desired ends. The criticisms of utilitarianism are, in the main, directed against its core idea that consequences are the exclusive determinate of the morality of our actions. Are there no other morally relevant constraints on our actions? In terms of outcomes, utilitarianism regards each individual recipient of benefit as equal to any other. Is an optimal distribution of good all that matters, or should we consider who deserves what? Can utilitarianism account for justice without an adequate conception of desert? Utilitarianism might be too demanding in that we are often incapable of foreseeing all the consequences of our actions and would nonetheless be held accountable for their outcomes, and demanding in the sense that it requires us to "bite the bullet" with respect to deeply held moral convictions or even sacrifice those dear to us or perhaps even ourselves for the sake of a greater good. Shouldn't an adequate moral theory allow us to act on our deepest convictions and treat ourselves and those close to us differently than we treat strangers? Utilitarianism eschews any substantive notion of obligation or duty. But mightn't we have general obligations and special obligations to certain individuals? Intentions and character have no place in a utilitarian calculation. We might, however, believe that these are greater determinants of the morality of our actions than consequences. We may have unique capacities and commitments. Should we give these up in favor of good outcomes? And finally utilitarianism holds us accountable for the consequences not only of our actions, but of our inaction and, in certain situations, even for the consequences of the actions of others, without any real distinction among these. Aren't we uniquely responsible for our own actions? Consideration of such questions points to some of the main problems with utilitarian moral theory. What follows is a brief summary of some central criticisms of that theory.

Utilitarianism is too demanding. There are several senses in which utilitarian is too demanding. In the first instance, it seems to require that we compute consequences for every action we take. Since actions are neither right nor wrong in themselves, actions are granted moral value only in terms of their results. But anything we do has the potential to generate good or bad consequences; therefore it would follow that any action, given a specific set of circumstances, can be morally right or morally wrong. If this were the case, we would be little more than consequence calculating devices. Following from this, we could never really be certain that the results we expect are those that will actually occur, and though it might be the case that acting on expected results is morally praiseworthy, it still may be possible that bad consequences result, in which case we would have acted badly and be held accountable for generating bad consequences. Here's a classic example of this: You save a drowning man with expected good consequences. The man you saved turns out to be Adolf Hitler. Wouldn't it have been better for the world to have let Hitler drown. There seems to be no assurance that we can get expected results and actual results to line up all the time. Moreover, utilitarianism is overly demanding in that it requires us to treat everyone with complete impartiality—no one, yourself, your family, your friends, counts any more or any less than anyone else. Each individual is counted simply as a neutral element in the consequentialist calculation. Think of the versions of the trolley problem where you can stop the trolley by jumping in front of it or stop it by directing it toward your aunt. In either case, it would seem utilitarianism requires you to do those things. Is it really possible to meet the requirement of complete impartiality under such circumstances?

Utilitarianism requires that we give up on certain fundamental moral concepts. The common conception of morality includes certain concepts that utilitarianism rejects—e.g., moral obligation, rights, and justice. Rejecting such concepts may lead to performing actions that are morally wrong, that violate fundamental rights, and that constitute or lead to serious injustices. Since no action is right or wrong in itself, it's possible that utilitarianism would require us to perform an action that the common conception of morality holds to be simply wrong—break a promise, kill an innocent person, steal another's property, etc. Under an ordinary view of morality, refraining from such actions is morally obligatory because they disrespect persons, infringe on a person's rights or otherwise violate some objective (or at least believed to be objective) moral principle. Think again of the doctor who kills the homeless man to harvest his organs for transplants. If the man has a right to life, then it is a clear violation of his rights to kill him. Rights impose constraints on our actions in the sense that possible courses of action, and hence some consequential outcomes, are morally unacceptable and thus ruled out. It is a serious injustice to use people as neutral devices in a consequentialist calculation, even if the results are optimal in that circumstance. Injustices may also follow from the utilitarian commitment to impartiality in outcomes. Is it simply the pattern of distribution that matters morally or does it make a difference who deserves to reap benefits and reward and who deserves ill? For the utilitarian it doesn't matter so long as the numbers work. No adequate moral theory should require morally wrong actions, violations of rights, and serious injustices. Utilitarianism might, at times, require these.

Utilitarianism adopts a notion of negative responsibility. This criticism comes from Bernard Williams's critique of utilitarianism.[5] Williams asks us to imagine the following scenario: Jim, a botanist, is on an expedition in a South American country. He stumbles upon a warlord, Pedro, who is about to kill twenty Indians. Pedro says to Jim if you shoot one Indian, I will let the other nineteen go. If Jim doesn't shoot the one, Pedro will shoot all twenty. What should Jim do? The ready-made utilitarian response is that, of course, Jim should shoot the one Indian, for in doing so he will have brought about better consequences than the alternative where Pedro shoots all twenty. What if Jim doesn't shoot the one Indian? Then, in some sense, utilitarianism holds him responsible. It's important to see just what this means. It's not merely that Jim would be responsible for the consequences of his inaction, as one might be if he did nothing to save a drowning baby. More than that Jim is responsible for the outcomes of an action that someone else performs. This seems to run completely counter to our ordinary notion of moral responsibility, which says we are accountable for our own actions and sometimes for omissions, but not that we are ever responsible for the outcomes of some other person's actions. Williams argues that consequentialism embraces a strong notion of negative responsibility; he defines negative responsibility in this way: "… if I know that if I do X, O_1 will eventuate, and if I refrain from doing X, O_2 will [eventuate], and that O_2 is worse than O_1, then I am responsible for O_2 if I refrain voluntarily from doing X."[6] It's one thing to say that Jim could have prevented the worse occurrence, but quite another to assert that he is responsible in the sense that his choice not to kill one Indian somehow made the worse occurrence happen. In the example, Pedro's actions—not Jim's inaction—directly produced the worse outcome. To hold Jim responsible in the same way is absurd. Utilitarianism cannot account for how it is that each of us is uniquely responsible for his or her actions and not responsible for the actions of others.

Utilitarianism violates personal integrity. This is also a major point in Williams's critique of utilitarianism.[7] Here is a simplified account of his concept of integrity. We have projects and deeply held commitments that define us as the kinds of persons we are and which motivate us to act. These projects and commitments have deep moral value for us and cannot be measured like pleasures in a utilitarian calculus nor understood from the perspective of utilitarian impartiality. Personal integrity is achieved in the pursuit of those projects and commitments. An adequate moral theory must take into account that one's projects and commitments have a normative dimension—think of the difference between Jim and Pedro, a botanist and a warlord—and that, most generally, one's actions need to be reflective of those projects and commitments. Utilitarianism requires Jim to act in a way inconsistent with his commitments, his most deeply held moral convictions. It requires him to give up on his personal moral commitments in favor of someone else's moral projects. Should we be required to do this whenever circumstances demand it? Utilitarianism suggests so. But this is the opposite of integrity. Integrity requires that people hold to their considered moral judgments and act in pursuit of their projects and commitments. Williams writes:

> *It is absurd to demand of such a man [i.e., a person who possesses integrity], when the sums come in from the utility network which the projects of others have in part determined, that he should just step aside from his own project and decision and acknowledge the decision which utilitarian calculation requires. It is to alienate him in a real sense from his actions and the source of his action in his own convictions. It is to make him into a channel between*

the input of everyone's projects, including his own, and an output of optimific decisions; but this is to neglect the extent to which his *actions and* his *decisions have to be seen as the actions and decisions which flow from the projects and attitudes with which he is most clearly identified. It is thus, in the most literal sense, an attack on his integrity.*[8]

Utilitarianism, then, with its emphasis on impartiality and its doctrine of negative responsibility divorces a person from his or her own moral convictions and places that person anywhere he or she might fit to meet the demands of a consequentialist calculation. This would be to deny any central role to integrity in the moral life.

A final thought about utilitarianism: What initially appears to be an elegantly simple idea about the purpose of morality—to make circumstances better for as many as possible—turns out to be extraordinarily complex and deeply flawed as a moral theory.

ENDNOTES

1. Jeremy Bentham, *Introduction to the Principles of Morals and Legislation* (Hafner, 1948), pp. 29–31. This work was originally published in 1789.
2. Bentham, p. 31.
3. The trolley problem was introduced by Phillipa Foot in her essay "The Problem of Abortion and the Doctrine of Double Effect" in *Virtues and Vices and Other Essays in Moral Philosophy* (Basil Blackwell, 1978). Judith Jarvis Thomson gives an extended analysis of this thought experiment in "The Trolley Problem" published in *The Yale Law Journal*, Vol. 94, No. 6 (May, 1985), pp. 1395–1415.
4. J. J. C. Smart, "An Outline of A System of Utilitarian Ethics" in J. J. C. Smart and Bernard Williams, *Utilitarinaism: For and Against,* (Cambridge University Press, 1973), pp. 3–74. See especially section 2 on act-utilitarianism and rule-utilitarianism, pp. 9–12. There Smart argues that rule-utilitarianism, in opting for rules over consequences, is a form of what he calls "rule worship".
5. Bernard Williams, "A Critique of Utilitarianism" in Smart and Williams, *Utilitarianism: For and Against,* pp. 77–150. See especially section 3 on negative responsibility, pp. 93–100.
6. Bernard Williams, p. 108.
7. See especially Williams on the concept of integrity, section 5 of his critique of utilitarianism, pp. 108–118.
8. Bernard Williams, pp. 116–117.

STUDY QUESTIONS

9. Distinguish between *consequentialism* and *deontology*.

10. In what sense is utilitarianism a consequentialist moral theory? Explain in detail how a utilitarian would decide whether or not an act is morally right?

11. What, according to utilitarianism, is the purpose of morality?

12. Explain the difference between *act-utilitarianism* and *rule-utilitarianism*.

13. Summarize the main arguments against utilitarianism.

14. What is the idea of *negative responsibility*? Consider the case of Jim and the Indians.

15. Describe Bernard Williams's idea of integrity.

QUESTIONS FOR REFLECTION

1. What is the *trolley problem*? Consider utilitarian responses to each of the following scenarios:
   a) pulling the switch and directing the trolley onto a side track, killing a person
   b) pushing a large person in front of the trolley
   c) jumping in front of the trolley yourself
   d) pulling the switch and directing the trolley onto a side track toward your aunt

   What would you do in each case? Give reasons for you answers.

2. Do you think we are ever responsible for the consequences of someone else's actions?

3. Utilitarianism embraces a strong notion of impartiality—everyone's interests count equally. If utilitarianism is true, then shouldn't we all sacrifice something to help anyone (those who are starving, for instance) in need? Or are we entitled to give greater weight to our own interests and those close to us? What do you think?

SUGGESTIONS FOR FURTHER READING

Bentham, Jeremy. *Introduction to the Principles of Morals and Legislation* [1789]. New York: Hafner, 1948.

Darwall, Stephen. *Consequentialism*. Oxford: Blackwell Publishing, 2003.

Eggleston, Ben & Miller, Dale E. eds. *The Cambridge Companion to Utilitarianism*. Cambridge: Cambridge University Press, 2014.

Foot, Philippa. "The Problem of Abortion and the Doctrine of Double Effect." *Oxford Review* 5, 1967.

Mill, John Stuart (Roger Crisp, ed.), *Utilitarianism* [1861]. Oxford: Oxford University Press, 1998.

Moore, G. E. *Principia Ethica* [1903]. Cambridge: Cambridge University Press, 1993.

Sidgwick, Henry. 1907. *The Methods of Ethics*, Seventh Edition [1907]. Indianapolis: Hackett Publishing Company, 1981.

Singer, Peter. "Famine, Affluence, and Morality." *Philosophy and Public Affairs*. 1(3), 1972.

Thomson, Judith Jarvis. "*The Trolley Problem*." 94 Yale Law Journal, 1985.

Williams, Bernard. "Persons, Character, and Morality," in Bernard Williams, *Moral Luck*. Cambridge: Cambridge University Press, 1981.

INDEX

U

Universalizability, Kantian principle of, 56, 64
Upanishads, 5
Utilitarianism, 38, 63, 75–76
    act-utilitarianism, 79–81
    consequentialism, 75, 76, 79
    criticisms of, 81–84
    decision-making, 77–79
    definition, 75
    and deontology, 64
    hedonistic, 75
    moral action, goal of, 75
    principle of, 80
    ready-made, 83
    rejection, 82
    rule-utilitarianism, 79–81
    serious flaws in, 81

V

Value pluralist, 41
Virtues
    application of, 71
    Aristotle's theory of. *See* Aristotle
    criticisms of, 70
    ethics, 63
    person, characteristics of, 66–68
    theory. *See* Aretaic ethics
    utilitarianism and Kantian deontology,
        70

W

Williams, Bernard, 83, 84
Worldview, 10

Printed in the USA
CPSIA information can be obtained
at www.ICGtesting.com
JSHW050838271223
R13205100001B/R132051PG54045JSX00001B/1

9 781524 917630